Service Learning for Health, Physical Education, and Recreation

A STEP-BY-STEP GUIDE

Cheryl Stevens, PhD
East Carolina University

Human Kinetics

Library of Congress Cataloging-in-Publication Data

Stevens, Cheryl A.
Service learning for health, physical education, and recreation : a step-by-step guide / Cheryl A. Stevens.
p. cm.
Includes bibliographical references and index.
ISBN-13: 978-0-7360-6022-6 (soft cover)
ISBN-10: 0-7360-6022-7 (soft cover)
1. Physical education and training--Curricula--Handbooks, manuals, etc. 2. Health education--Curricula--Handbooks, manuals, etc. 3. Recreation--Curricula--Handbooks, manuals, etc. 4. Service learning--Handbooks, manuals, etc. 5. Student volunteers in social service--Handbooks, manuals, etc. I. Title.
GV365.S57 2008
796.071--dc22

2008022751

ISBN-10: 0-7360-6022-7
ISBN-13: 978-0-7360-6022-6

The Web addresses cited in this text were current as of June 10, 2008, unless otherwise noted.

Acquisitions Editor: Gayle Kassing, PhD; **Developmental Editor:** Jacqueline Eaton Blakley; **Assistant Editors:** Bethany J. Bentley and Lauren B. Morenz; **Copyeditor:** Erich Shuler; **Proofreader:** Kathy Bennett; **Indexer:** Ann W. Truesdale; **Permission Manager:** Dalene Reeder; **Graphic Designer:** Fred Starbird; **Graphic Artist:** Denise Lowry; **Cover Designer:** Bob Reuther; **Photographer (cover):** Philip Lee Harvey/Getty Images; **Photo Asset Manager:** Laura Fitch; **Visual Production Assistant:** Joyce Brumfield; **Photo Office Assistant:** Jason Allen; **Printer:** Versa Press

Printed in the United States of America 10 9 8 7 6 5 4 3 2 1

Human Kinetics
Web site: www.HumanKinetics.com

United States: Human Kinetics, P.O. Box 5076, Champaign, IL 61825-5076
800-747-4457
e-mail: humank@hkusa.com

Canada: Human Kinetics, 475 Devonshire Road Unit 100, Windsor, ON N8Y 2L5
800-465-7301 (in Canada only)
e-mail: info@hkcanada.com

Europe: Human Kinetics, 107 Bradford Road, Stanningley, Leeds LS28 6AT, United Kingdom
+44 (0) 113 255 5665
e-mail: hk@hkeurope.com

Australia: Human Kinetics, 57A Price Avenue, Lower Mitcham, South Australia 5062
08 8372 0999
e-mail: info@hkaustralia.com

New Zealand: Human Kinetics, Division of Sports Distributors NZ Ltd., P.O. Box 300 226 Albany, North Shore City, Auckland
0064 9 448 1207
e-mail: info@humankinetics.co.nz

This book is dedicated to
every person who is willing
to change the world by
engaging in consequential
acts of service.

Contents

Step 3
Planning the Project

Step 4
Implementing the Plan

Step 5
Finishing the Project

Preface

The teacher wasn't sure what to do. The health fair was just a week away, and only a few students were taking their preparations for it seriously. Some students were working around the clock, while others didn't seem to care. The teacher was putting in 70 hours a week, and she felt that things were out of control. She realized, *If I don't step in, this health fair will be a disaster.*

After the fair, it was evident that only a couple of students and the teacher had done most of the work. The teacher asked herself, *What's the point of service learning if I'm the one running the project?* She knew that service learning was valuable, but she realized that something had to be done differently.

The next year, things changed. Team building was done early. The students decided that they would divide into smaller groups according to tasks. Timelines were established, and each group discussed its progress on a weekly basis. The next health fair was still hectic, but everyone pitched in. There was no last-minute panic, and at the end of the class, everyone celebrated a successful event. Upon reflection, the teacher realized that the students who were not doing their share of the work the previous year were not necessarily lazy; they just didn't know what to do, or they didn't understand how far in advance they needed to begin preparing.

Large class projects have a way of turning enthusiastic students and teachers into disenchanted ones, and that certainly can be the case with service-learning projects. Although such projects offer unique opportunities for students to put their classroom lessons into practice, to deal with real people and real problems and to feel the joy of helping others, they're challenging to execute. In most cases, service-learning projects require multiple tasks, long-term efforts, and extraordinary commitment. This book gives your class the tools to prevent common problems and to deal constructively with difficulties.

This book's step-by-step process guides high school and university students in health, physical education, and recreation classes through an easy-to-follow, practical process for completing complex service-learning projects. The five-step process moves from determining the group's functions to planning, implementing, and evaluating the service project. The tools, techniques, and resources in this book will help you minimize frustration while maximizing the quality of your service programs.

Your class can customize the process to your service project by completing the included activities. The activities will teach you about group dynamics, communication skills, leadership, planning, problem solving, service, evaluation, and reflection. Each student will learn how to take responsibility for the project. Thus students and teachers can avoid common problems such as a lack of clarity about goals and roles, certain students doing more work than others, teachers doing work that the students should be doing, negative group dynamics, poor communication, students not completing tasks, excessive stress, a lack of a clear connection between project and educational objectives, and a lack of time for adequate reflection. While most teachers of health, physical education, and recreation classes believe in the value of service learning, many are reluctant to make a commitment to a project, because of these potential problems.

This book is the result of my three years of reflection in action while conducting complex service-learning projects at the college level. I've drawn on 20 years of experiential education, organizational development, and teaching in secondary schools and colleges to create this practical process, which has been tested and proved by other teachers. While many anecdotes about successful service-learning projects exist, this book is the first to provide a practical, yet theory-based approach.

Service learning is best when it's student-centered. This book provides students and teachers with a method for determining how to act, what to do when, and how to make sure that everyone in the class contributes their unique skills. As with all learning, it is up to the students to maximize the value of each project through their commitment. My hope is that this book will help each reader contribute to a meaningful service project that teaches them about leadership, group process, commitment, and class content while experiencing the fulfillment that comes from helping others.

Acknowledgments

There are many people who have directly influenced the writing of this book. Some provided behind-the-scenes support; others were teachers on a more personal level. I will thank them here chronologically, in the hope that I can include all those whose knowledge and expertise contributed so significantly to this project.

I trace my knowledge roots in outdoor leadership, student-centered learning, and organizational development to three influential mentors. "Charlie" Mand, former director of the school of HPER at Ohio State University, gave me the opportunity to become an outdoor leader and earn a PhD. Sy Kleinman, professor emeritus at OSU, was my first truly student-centered teacher and the catalyst for my quest to become a master learner. Connie Phillips, organizational development specialist for the City of Anaheim, helped me discover the simple truisms of "what always works" in performance management and team development.

My best teachers have, of course, been my students. I'd like to thank those directly responsible for this book. Students in my 1996 and 1997 conference planning seminar classes at SUNY Cortland inspired and tested these tips, tools, and techniques. And they, along with students at the City of Anaheim and East Carolina University, have patiently shown me over the years the value of service learning and student-centered education. I'd also like to thank my colleagues, Rachelle Toupence and Susan Wilson, who further tested my ideas in their classes.

I have a deep sense of gratitude for all the writers listed in the references who took the time to relate their insights, and I admire their discipline and dedication. Furthermore, Gayle Kassing, Jackie Blakley, and the staff at Human Kinetics provided the faith, editing, and reminders necessary to bring the book from idea to reality.

On a personal note, there are significant others for whom I have a deep, abiding appreciation. My mother, Jeralyn Rae (Stevens) Arnold, and father, William Carroll Arnold, whose unconditional love allowed me to take risks. My daughters Katherine (partner in personal growth) and Erin (teacher of self-assurance), because without them life wouldn't be the same. All those teachers, too numerous to name, who helped me learn what works and what doesn't work by providing the lessons I needed when I needed them. My mentor and friend, Erica Petrullo, who provided the gentle guidance I needed to locate the intrinsic motivation necessary to complete this project. And both last and first, Douglas Lamont, my ultimate playmate, whose love, intellect, humor, creativity, and unwavering support made this (and all future projects) more joyful.

Introduction

All genuine education comes about through experience.

—John Dewey

You're about to discover that moving out of the classroom and serving others is a powerful and enduring learning experience. Service learning is a hands-on class project in which you learn while helping others, discover how class knowledge is useful in the real world, master practical skills (such as project management, leadership, teamwork, and communication), and gain an appreciation for diversity, civic responsibility, and service. You can expect to have fun too! It is a joy to be a part of a self-directed team that can complete a challenging project and thereby help others. There is a strong relationship between play and learning; service learning is as fun as it is educational.

Service-learning projects are complicated; overcoming the challenges that are inherent in such projects is a big part of what makes them such a powerful learning experience. Risk, challenge, and even a certain amount of frustration are required for students to grow. This book will guide you through this learning process.

WHAT IS SERVICE LEARNING?

John Dewey once said that people don't learn from experience but from *processing* their experiences. Therefore, a period of reflection is built in to every service-learning project. Service learning is somewhat different from volunteer work. It is a class-based, credit-bearing experience in which students participate in an organized service activity that meets a particular need of a community. A period of structured reflection facilitates the understanding of course content and of civic responsibility (adapted from Hamner 2002). What makes a class project a true service-learning experience, as opposed to a volunteering or community-service experience? In short: learning outcomes, reflection, and reciprocity.

Learning Outcomes

During a service-learning project, you will be expected to apply what you are learning in class to a real-world, hands-on project. Your teacher will explain how to apply, and to expand on, course content. You and your teacher have a shared responsibility to articulate, before the service project begins, the theory-into-practice lessons that you are expected to learn. In some cases, the teacher will determine the learning outcomes ahead of time. In other cases, you, the students, will be given a chance to contribute. In either case, it's important to review the learning outcomes so that you have ownership of the experience. Once you know the learning outcomes, you will be able to recognize spontaneous learning opportunities as they arise. Activities in steps 1 and 3 will guide you and your classmates through the writing and refining of your learning-outcomes statements.

Reflection

Genuine reflection is the key to service learning, so consider it a vital, ongoing process. Certain methods of reflection—such as doing structured activities, having guided discussions, and keeping a journal—are more formal. Journaling instructions are included in step 1. At other times, reflection occurs spontaneously. There are suggested short, spontaneous reflection activities at the end of each step. At the end of the project, most students will be asked to write a reflection paper or to give a presentation. You will by guided through a natural thinking process that follows a pattern of reflective thinking and action. You will be asked to answer the questions "What?" "So what?" and "Now what?" These questions help you think about what has happened, what effect it has had, and what to do next. This process can be used by an individual or by a group. Expect questions to look something like this:

1. What has happened to me, the class, or the service project?
2. What do these events mean, and how do I feel about them?
3. Based on my answers to questions 1 and 2, how can I apply what I have learned?

Reciprocity

Reciprocity in a relationship happens when people exchange something of value with each other. For example, recreation students can learn about leading games as they help children in afterschool programs feel a sense of belonging to a group. In this sense, service learning is a win-win proposition for students and communities. Students have talents, skills, and information that communities need. The community offers opportunities for students to learn from experience, which is the best way to learn.

AP Images/Stephen Morton

A project that addresses authentic community need is likely to engender genuine enthusiasm.

For service learning to be of value, a community's needs must be evaluated carefully. If you don't engage with a community in a way that meets its needs, then much may happen, but little will be accomplished.

A HIGH-QUALITY SERVICE-LEARNING EXPERIENCE

Not all service-learning projects are equally educational. Before you begin a project, you need to understand the conditions that determine whether a service-learning experience will be successful. As educational philosopher John Dewey notes, an experience is educational when it is of good quality, when it engages the learner, and when there is continuity with the student's future experiences. It is also important to understand various approaches and attitudes toward learning in order to get the most out of service-learning experiences.

A high-quality service-learning project is well planned. Planning requires communicating early on with potential partners as well as taking the following steps:

- Clarifying community and class needs
- Defining goals
- Describing roles
- Planning a step-by-step implementation process
- Securing supervision and guidance
- Setting up support systems that will ensure timely feedback and possible course corrections
- Planning enough time for reflection and evaluation

Good planning and ongoing care of the service project are essential. If your team follows the steps and troubleshooting guides in this book, you will be able to avoid many typical pitfalls, and you will know how to deal with problems when they arise.

Service learning is particularly appealing to health, physical education, and recreation classes. In these disciplines, it is not enough to earn an A on a test; students must know how to apply their knowledge in order to help people in need. The following examples of service-learning projects may help you understand this idea.

- As part of a health education class, service-learning students traveled to a low-income rural community in order to train women in that community to be peer educators for improved breast health. As a result of the campaign and of continued peer support, many women in that community received early treatment that may have saved their lives. The students learned this valuable lesson: "When you give a person a fish, he eats for a day; when you teach a person to fish, he eats for a lifetime."

- As part of a physical education measurement class, students partnered with a local elementary school that had never before participated in the Presidential Physical Fitness Testing Program. The students not only planned and conducted the program but they also designed and completed a research project for physical fitness testing. In addition to providing a valuable service to the elementary school, the students gained hands-on experience with physical fitness testing, data collection, analysis, and reporting.

• College seniors, as part of a recreation and leisure studies course, traveled regularly to a rural elementary school that had been devastated by a flood. They started a mentoring program that used character-building recreational activities for students in the afterschool program. These students learned firsthand about the challenges that minority children in poor, rural areas face every day. They also learned how to design and implement programs that improve children's lives.

BENEFITS OF SERVICE LEARNING

Service-learning experiences have multiple, proven benefits for students, teachers, communities, and learning institutions. Since service learning requires a great deal of effort from everyone involved, participants in a project can find motivation by learning about the potential benefits of a project before beginning it.

Benefits to Students

Service-learning projects allow students to develop in numerous ways that can have lifelong benefits. First, gaining practical experience puts education theory into practice and thereby makes it more relevant. Practical experience also allows people to learn in a variety of ways (Lee, Bush, and Smith 2005). Furthermore, real-world learning prepares you for further education, for careers, and for community involvement. It is difficult to overestimate the value of learning by doing. Students who transition well from high school to college and from college to the workplace are those who switch from being receivers of information to being seekers of information; they take responsibility for their learning. A student at the University of Minnesota (n.d.) recalls, "Service learning has given me the opportunity to give theory value and significance outside of the classroom. Through service learning, I have had to keep my books and mind open indefinitely. This is one of the most important lessons to be learned in life."

Second, those who engage in service learning tend to be more satisfied with their lives. Serving others makes the server feel good. Volunteer work has been found to enhance five aspects of personal well-being: happiness, life satisfaction, sense of control over life, physical health, and positive mood (Thoits and Hewitt 2001). Those who engage in shared tasks such as community service feel greater life satisfaction, personal control, vitality, and social support later in life (Harlow and Cantor 1996). At Arizona State University (n.d.), a student said, "I have never been more involved in the community than I am now. I am very grateful because service learning has taught me a great lesson in humility and kindness towards my fellow man and especially children."

Third, service learning has been shown to enhance knowledge and skills and to improve self-esteem when students enter the workforce (Higgs, cited in Lee, Bush, and Smith 2005). A National Commission on Service Learning report (2002) documented the benefits of service learning to K-12 students. Benefits included improvements in academic achievement, problem-solving skills, character, and social behavior. Additional benefits include being exposed to new careers, feeling stronger community ties, and feeling a desire for continued civic engagement. One student intern described the benefits he received in this way: "Service learning has more than proved itself to me to be a great experience for anyone. The communication and problem-solving skills it forces you to sharpen are valuable to anyone in any career . . . I will use the skills I learned this semester for the rest of my life" (Arizona State University n.d.).

Benefits to the Community and to the Educational Institution

Evidence shows that service learning is highly valued and that it is supported by governments, communities, and schools. Approximately $40 million in grants was made available through the Corporation for National and Community Service (n.d.). The money was used to support service-learning projects for school-based, community-based, higher-education programs, as well as for tribal and U.S. territory programs in 2006 to 2007. Dr. William Richardson, president and CEO of the W.K. Kellogg Foundation (n.d.), believes that service learning improves communities because it fosters students' sense of civic responsibility and their commitment to community involvement.

Communities and educational institutions openly value, support, and often reward those who work together to meet community needs. Today's universities have been criticized for being out of touch, out of date, and unresponsive to society's needs (Kellogg Commission 1999). Service learning, however, is a way for universities to meet a community's needs by combining students and academic resources to address local problems.

Community agencies and community members benefit in a number of ways from service-learning partnerships. Many community agencies have too few resources to provide adequate services. Volunteers help these agencies, but service-learners are more than volunteers. In addition to improving an agency's productivity, students can provide agencies with new knowledge, publicity, and evaluative reports; they might be able to arrange for access to campus facilities and resources; and they can help with grant-writing efforts.

In the words of noted anthropologist Margaret Mead, "Never doubt that a small group of thoughtful, committed citizens can change the world. Indeed, it's the only thing that ever has."

FIVE-STEP PROCESS FOR SUCCESSFUL SERVICE-LEARNING PROJECTS

Positive service-learning experiences require personal investment, insight, and planning. The five-step process outlined in this workbook (see the chart on this page for a visual overview) will guide and structure your efforts. The tools, techniques, and tips can be customized to fit your project. One of the difficulties with service learning is not knowing what factors you should plan for. By following the activities in this book, you can develop your team as you develop your plan. You can avoid pitfalls by learning from what others have already gone through. This will save you from having to do a lot of outside research. Each stage of the process also contains a troubleshooting checklist that will help you determine which tools you should use to address problems.

Step 1: Launching the Project

The first requirement for launching a successful service-learning project is to choose the best

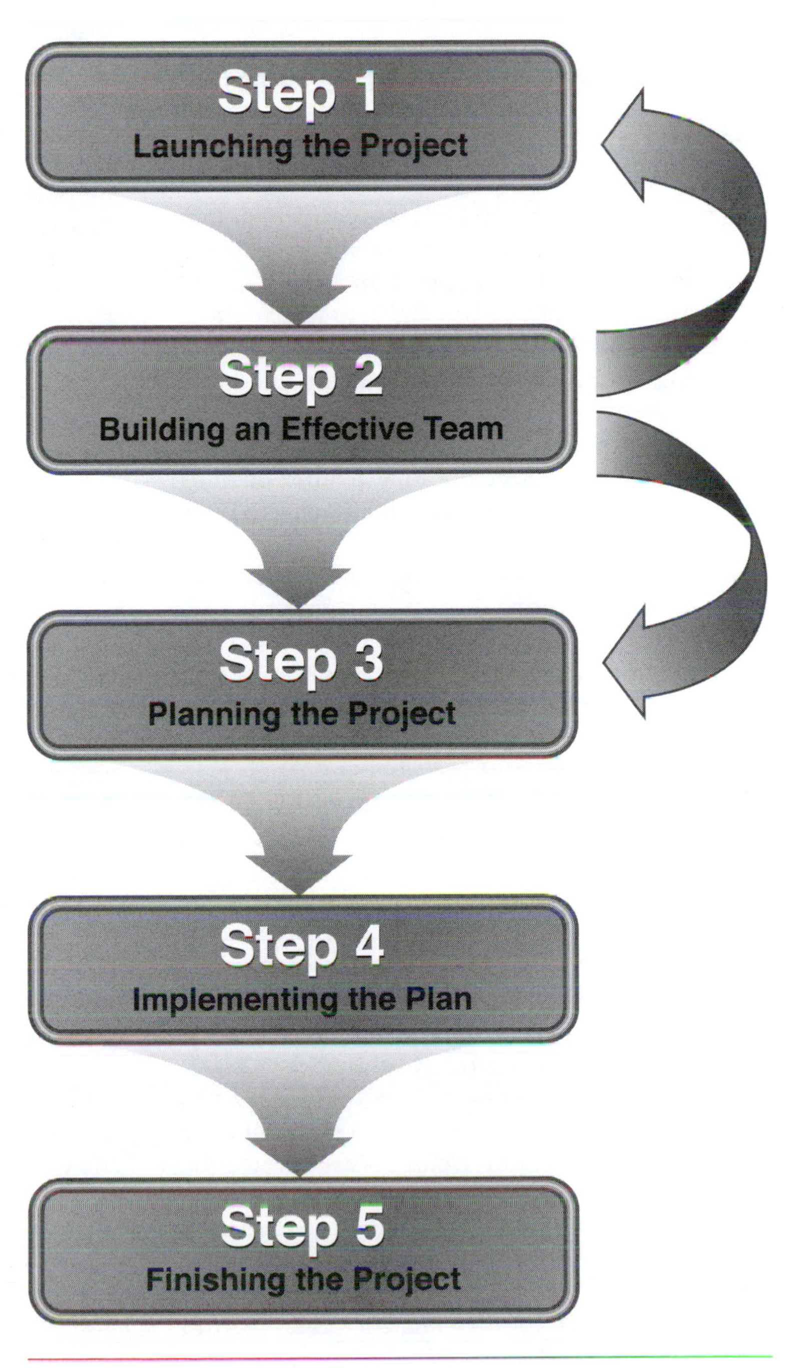

Overview of the five steps of a service-learning project.

possible project. When there are time constraints, the teacher typically chooses the project. When time permits, students might be allowed more input in choosing the projects. Either way, the activities in this chapter are critical for maximizing your learning opportunities and for building relationships with the people you will serve. Your team will work on steps 1 and 2 simultaneously because you can do the team building when you are not meeting with agencies and clients.

Step 2: Building an Effective Team

Building an effective team is the ounce of prevention that's worth a pound of cure. Students often complain that they don't enjoy group projects because only a few people end up doing most of the work. Though there are slackers in any class, it is more often the case that these students are not doing their share because they are uncertain of what they should do and why they should do it. Step 2 features several exercises that will help your class learn about positive team dynamics and will ensure that your class functions as a high-performance team.

Organizational behavior specialists know that effective teams must buy in and commit to a project and understand the ground rules. They should also be able to solve problems, give and receive feedback, conduct meetings, and understand group dynamics and leadership. These skills can help your group succeed; they also will help prepare you for life. Good teamwork and leadership skills are essential in any work environment.

Step 3: Planning the Project

In this step, you will learn about the needs of the people you will serve. Once your needs assessment is complete, your team can prepare a mission statement and write goals. Your teacher will help you clarify how the project's goals fit with the class's learning outcomes. Then you will be ready to design tasks, action plans, and timelines, and to visually depict task pathways so that each student can see how his individual tasks and deadlines will contribute to the overall project. By this point, each of you will have a clear picture of your roles, deadlines, and resources.

Step 4: Implementing the Plan

Next you will use a step-by-step approach to implement the plan for your service-learning project. Expect your teacher to facilitate regular periods of reflection through activities such as group discussions and journaling. Reflection throughout the process is essential for learning and for the success of the project. At some point after beginning their tasks, each student subgroup will report back to the group in order to gauge the group's progress and to make necessary adjustments. Good communication and effective group meetings are essential for successful service projects. Good time management, focus, accountability, and the giving and receiving of feedback will also help. Using the group-process skills you learned in step 2, your class can maintain a strong sense of mission, resolve conflicts, reinforce expectations, and keep your morale high. As the project draws to a close, you will ask for feedback on the project from the people you have served. This will help you celebrate your successes and learn from your mistakes, and it will provide you with food for thought as you move into the final step.

Step 5: Finishing the Project

In your project timeline, time has been set aside for class debriefing, reflection, and celebration when the project is complete. If the project is to be continued by new students at some point in the future, you can prepare records and resources now so that those students will learn from, and then add to, what you learned. In your final evaluation, you will complete a self-assessment and you will receive an evaluation from your teacher. You will conclude with a structured reflection on what you have learned: What new knowledge, skills, and attitudes have you gained? By reflecting on what you have accomplished and learned, you will make connections and generate insights that will help you in the future.

You are probably used to teachers directing your learning. Well, get ready to take ownership and responsibility for your learning through meaningful service. Remember, the quality of your learning is only as good as your personal investment. If you are to learn from your project, it must be you, the students, who do the project, not the teacher. Your teacher's role is to instruct and guide you, not to do the project for you. The more you invest, the more you will gain.

UNDERSTANDING ROLES

Knowing your role before you start a project is critical for service-learning success. Everyone must know his or her role, including students and teachers, as well as agencies such as community groups and educational institutions.

The roles of students and teachers in a service-learning class are somewhat different than in the typical teacher-centered, authority-based classroom. In a service-learning class, both students and teachers are equally responsible for the project's success. Paulo Freier (2000), a strong advocate for students and teachers working in partnership, explains that through regular dialogue the distinction between teacher and students becomes less and less because teachers and students are learning from each other when everyone is jointly responsible for learning and growing. Students, not teachers, should be at the center of the service-learning process. Teachers *are* learners in the group; they just happen to be the more-experienced learners. And, of course, they are in charge of leading the process. If the teacher leads well, however, the students will feel as though they've achieved success by themselves.

Agencies include community groups and educational institutions. Understanding the roles they play in service learning will help students interact effectively with these groups. Although the roles and tasks are precisely explained in step 1, an overview is important for understanding how each partner's role fits into the bigger picture.

AP Images/Mary Altaffer

It's your responsibility to maintain a positive attitude throughout your project.

The Role of Students

Students need to understand that they are expected to take initiative and interact with others during the project. Students are expected to do the following:

- Get excited about hands-on learning and helping others.
- Take responsibility for, and ownership of, their learning process.
- Put genuine effort into the steps that are outlined in this workbook.
- Keep an open mind and a positive attitude, and be willing to ask appropriate questions.
- Expect difficulties and conflicts, and commit to working through them.
- Maintain the utmost respect and professionalism toward classmates, teachers, and community members.
- When you are working on a task for the project, give 100 percent of your effort to the task. Be a person they can count on to do what is needed and to do it right.

Note that all of the items in the list require you to have a positive attitude. A self-evaluation form is introduced in step 3. Knowing in advance that you are accountable to yourself, your classmates, and your teacher will make it easier to take personal responsibility and to take a positive approach to the service-learning project.

The Role of Teachers

Teachers have to learn to not do too much. A teacher's role will involve teaching, planning, coaching, supporting, and facilitating reflection.

Teachers are expected to do the following:

- Design the class learning outcomes and projects, and grade students according to their achievement.
- Involve students in assessing community

needs and in choosing the service-learning project. If students can't choose the site, make sure that they decide on as many key elements as possible (such as project mission).

- Help students connect what they learn in class with what they learn through the service-learning project.
- Spend time at the community site and ask questions. For example, will students provide direct services or indirect services? What are their hours? Are there opportunities for the students to lead? Will the students be adequately supervised?
- Maintain a balance between leading tasks, coaching, participating, and delegating. Students can be given more independence once they demonstrate that they can handle it. A skilled teacher will solve problems with the students rather than fix things for them.
- Provide relevant diversity training and solicit student feedback about the sites they visit.
- Be prepared to serve as an organization development specialist, resource provider, coach, and feedback specialist.
- Design and schedule in periods of reflection. Reflection will help students use what they are learning in other areas of their lives.

Teachers should expect to be most directive early in the service-learning process. As students gain experience and confidence, teachers can step back and assume the roles of coach, teacher, co–problem solver, and resource person. Teachers will make structured reflection a priority, so be prepared to have your teacher tell you to complete journals and other reflection activities.

The Role of Agencies

For a service-learning project to be successful, a community agency must work effectively with students and their teacher. Agency members must be genuinely interested in receiving services from students and in taking an active role in the students' learning.

The agency is expected to do the following:

- Allow teachers and students to talk to the people they will be serving in order to figure out what they need and want.
- Receive students openly and warmly when they visit the agency to learn about the community.
- Ensure that students have plenty of direct interaction with the clients.
- Provide adequate hours and supervision for the students to interact with the clients.
- Provide an honest evaluation of the project: what was done well, and what could have been done better.
- Celebrate successes with the students.

Not all agencies have the ability or willingness to invest this kind of time and energy in working with students. Many agencies want student volunteers to help out, but not all of them are aware that they should be active partners in service learning. As you plan your project, you will make sure that the agency knows what you expect from them as well as what they can expect from you.

The Role of Educational Institutions

Schools and universities should be supportive partners in service learning. A quick Internet search for "service-learning successes" will reveal hundreds of examples of what schools are doing to support service learning. The following are things that schools can do to support service-learning projects:

- Publicly state the connections between service learning and the mission of the educational institution.
- Recognize and reward outstanding students, teachers, projects, and community agency partners.
- Allow teachers to adjust their teaching loads and to teach smaller classes in order to allow for the extra time commitment that service learning requires.
- As the number of service-learning projects grows, commit to joining organizations such as Campus Compact and to administering service-learning efforts; commit also to faculty training, liability insurance, transportation, and minigrants.
- Ask the school's public relations employee to generate positive press for service-learning projects.

Service-Learning Resources

Campus Compact is a national coalition of more than 1,100 college and university presidents—representing some 6 million students—dedicated to promoting community service, civic engagement, and service learning in higher education. Go to www.campuscompact.org to access their network of information and resources.

Learn and Serve America is a program of the Corporation for National and Community Service. Go to www.learnandserve.gov to access their vast clearinghouse of information designed for service-learning students at all educational levels.

Learning In Deed is a resource site supported by the W.K. Kellogg Foundation to promote service-learning in K-12 education. Go to http://learningindeed.org/index.html in order to access information on grants, tools and resources, as well as research.

Every day more schools and universities are getting involved in service learning. Learn and Serve America, a branch of the Corporation for National and Community Service (n.d.), provides grants and support materials for numerous school- and university-based service-learning projects. There are more than 950 college and university members of Campus Compact—representing some 6 million students—who are dedicated to promoting community service, civic engagement, and service learning in higher education (see the service-learning resources).

While you, the students, are at the center of the service-learning world, you are not in it alone. Teachers work to maintain a balance among teaching, leading tasks, coaching, participating, and delegating. Your school should provide resources such as facilities, insurance, transportation, equipment, and sometimes funding. Motivated community groups will establish positive relationships with your class while providing varied, meaningful service opportunities for students. Knowing what kind of partners you want to work with will help ensure that your service-learning experience is a positive one.

SUMMARY

Ultimately, service-learning magic occurs when the partners in a project are committed to making a difference in people's lives, to learning, and to putting in the physical, emotional, and mental effort to move forward even when faced with difficulties. Many of the skills that you need in order to succeed at service learning—education, diversity, teamwork, communication, and project management—will benefit you as a lifelong learner and future citizen. Nothing substitutes for hands-on experience. It gives you, the students, an advantage in future workplaces (Hamner 2002).

You are about to begin a complex service-learning project that, with proper planning and commitment, will pay dividends that far exceeds your investment. Expect your service-learning experience to be about both process and product. Keep your focus on both, because in life beyond the classroom, one does not succeed without the other.

Step 1 will help your class become a strong team. You will simultaneously learn and use the skills you'll need for continued success, and that will make your hands-on learning relevant.

REFERENCES

Arizona State University. n.d. *Academic community engagement services: The service learning program.* http://universitycollege.asu.edu/servicelearning.

Corporation for National and Community Service. n.d. About us and our programs. www.nationalservice.org.

Dewey, J. 1938/1988. Experience and education. In J.A. Boydston and B. Levine (Eds.), *John Dewey: The later works, 1925-1953: Vol. 13. 1938-1939* (pp. 1-62). Carbondale: Southern Illinois University Press.

Freire, P. 2000. *Pedagogy of the oppressed* [trans. by Merna Bergman Ramos]. New York: Continuum.

Hamner, D.M. 2002. Building bridges: The Allyn & Bacon student guide to service-learning. Needham Heights, MA: Allyn & Bacon.

Harlow, R.E., and N. Cantor. 1996. Still participating after all these years: A study of task participation in later life. *Journal of Personality and Social Psychology 71*(6), pp. 1235–1249.

Kellogg Commission on the Future of State and Land Grant Universities. 1999. *Returning to our roots: The engaged institution* (third report). Washington, DC: National Association of State Universities and Land Grant Colleges.

Lee, J.W., G. Bush, and E.W. Smith. 2005. Service learning: Practical experiences in sport and physical education. *Strategies 18*(3), pp. 11-13.

Thoits, P.A., and L.N. Hewitt. 2001. Volunteer work and well-being. *Journal of Health and Social Behavior 42*(2), 115-131.

University of Minnesota. n.d. Career and community learning center: Community involvement and service learning. www.servicelearning.umn.edu.

W.K. Kellogg Foundation. n.d. Learning in deed. http://learningindeed.org.

STEP

Launching the Project

Step 5
Finishing the Project

Step 4
Implementing the Plan

Step 3
Planning the Project

Step 2
Building an Effective Team

Step 1
Launching the Project

In this step you will

- **identify clients with real and important needs,**
- **visit agencies and choose one to contract, and**
- **get started on journals.**

There are three ways of trying to win the young. There is persuasion, there is compulsion, and there is attraction. You can preach at them; that is a hook without a worm. You can say, "You must volunteer." That is the devil. And you can tell them, "You are needed." That hardly ever fails.

—Kurt Hahn

People are motivated when they know they are needed. As you plan your service-learning project, you will discover how great the service needs are in your community. You will make connections with people who will show you that you are needed. A solid foundation for your service-learning project is essential if the project is to run smoothly. Prepare the foundation for your project by determining the following:

- What your class is supposed to learn during the project
- The scope of what your class can (and can't) do
- Which project is the best one to take on
- How to establish solid relationships with clients through personal contact

This step first describes the qualities of a good service-learning project. Then it outlines what your class should do when selecting an agency partner. Next you will plan for site visits and engage in contracting. (*Contracting* is the process of finalizing commitments and making a formal agreement with an agency about what your class will do and what you expect from the agency.) When you visit an agency, you should establish relationships with your clients. (The word *clients* refers to the people you are helping. You may choose to think of them in some other way, depending on what best suits your situation.) During the contracting process, you should get to know your clients personally. This will help them feel as committed to the project as you do. You also will learn about how they will fulfill their part of the partnership.

The word *partnership* implies that at least two parties are involved. Your class does not just do something *for* someone; your class works *with* someone. Communication is the key to all successful partnerships. Therefore, once you begin working with clients, do not assume anything; there are questions to ask, and there is information that both partners need to know up front. I can't overemphasize how important direct communication is. It will be necessary for making appointments and for visiting your clients face to face.

In some cases you may be planning an event for which there is no permanent program site, such as a 5K running venue. Whatever your situation, you will need to communicate directly with your clients in order to clarify who will do what, when they will do it, and why they will do it. If you have any fears about visiting sites and talking with clients, prepare to get over them. Get ready to make those visits.

When step 1 is complete, you will know a lot about your project and about your clients. You will understand why you are needed and how, by meeting the needs of your clients, you will learn something valuable. Because the activities in step 1 will progress, in part, according to the schedules of the class and the agency, your teacher might have you start on step 2, Building an Effective Team, at the same time that you are completing step 1.

QUALITIES OF A GOOD SERVICE-LEARNING PROJECT

Determining whether a potential service-learning opportunity is a good fit for your class can be complicated. There's more to finding a good service-learning project than just locating an agency that needs volunteers. A poor project fit can result in a neutral effect (when students remain unaffected by the experience) or a negative effect (when students learn the wrong lesson or reinforce negative stereotypes). According to Mark Cooper (n.d.), coordinator of Florida International University's Volunteer Action Center, three things can happen when students get involved in community service:

> First and foremost, students can learn something about themselves, about their community, and about pressing social issues. Second, students can learn nothing. A group can feed the homeless yet remain unaffected by the experience. Third, students can learn the wrong lesson—prejudices and stereotypes can be reinforced or created while on a poorly planned service outing. (p. 4)

The key to a good service-learning experience is getting to know your project and your clients early. Keep the following characteristics of successful service-learning projects in mind. These will help you have a good attitude about your project (Learn and Serve America Clearinghouse n.d.):

- All partners are committed to a shared vision.
- Student-learning outcomes are compatible with the service to be performed.
- Agendas and needs are openly expressed, and while they are probably not identical, they are at least compatible.
- Partners are sensitive to the needs, styles, and limitations of others.
- Among individuals of all levels, there will be frequent and open communication, especially about goals, tasks, roles, and accountability.

AP Images/The Town Talk, Tia Owens-Powers

Most service-learning projects in health, physical education, and recreation involve helping people directly.

Another characteristic of successful service-learning projects is direct service. Most service-learning projects in health, physical education, and recreation help people directly. Direct service involves mentoring, teaching, coaching, special events, or leading programs. A direct service project that is well suited to service learning has the following qualities:

- There are plenty of opportunities for *every* student to interact directly with the clients.
- The clients appreciate that the students have performed a meaningful service for them.
- There is enough meaningful work for every student to do.

Since it is important for *every* student to interact directly with the clients, you and your teacher should decide whether to target one agency that serves a lot of clients or whether a collaborative projects approach would make more sense. A single service project makes sense when there are a lot of tasks to accomplish and a lot of clients to work with. But if that type of project is not available, a collaborative project approach may work better. This can be achieved in two ways. The first is by working with multiple agencies to increase the number of roles for students, thereby exposing them to clients with different needs. The second way is to divide a large class into small groups—for instance, by dividing a class of 24 students into three groups of eight. The objectives and scope of each group's project would be the same, but there would be more opportunities for students to interact directly with clients, and there would be plenty of work for everyone. Here are some examples of collaborative projects; one of these approaches might be a good fit for your class:

- A therapeutic recreation class is doing a service-learning project over two semesters. They are working with mentally retarded and developmentally disabled adults. In addition to raising funds, they are cooking dinner for another local agency that hosted a Friday Night Supper for people living in poverty. In this example, students benefit from interacting with various types of clients, and the clients benefit from the interactions of various community groups. Another idea is to have seniors interact with young children in a day care program; seniors often value opportunities for companionship, and young children need to have positive interactions with adults.

- A leisure philosophy class of 30 students is divided into groups of three to five students. Each group of students identifies its own clients. Each group customizes its leisure education programs based on its clients' leisure needs. Students work with diverse groups, such as homebound elderly seniors, children with special needs, family members, and even other college students. Each service project has the same learning outcomes, but the way that students shape each project depends on each client's needs.

Service-learning projects can also deliver indirect services; that is, students are not directly involved with the people they are serving. Examples of indirect service include environmental cleanup and grant writing. Health, recreation, and physical education are hands-on professions. Service-learning projects in these areas—projects that include direct interaction with clients—tend to provide the most learning opportunities. In cases where the client's need is great, and where you feel that that need is important, indirect service may make sense if it fits your class' learning outcomes. For example, a class on research and evaluation may choose to evaluate a program for an agency (indirect service) rather than directly deliver the program.

Here are some ideas for direct-service programs in health, physical education, and recreation. Most of these programs can be used with people of all ages. Also consider using these programs with groups who have special needs, such as persons with physical or mental impairments, or with those who are considered at risk due to socioeconomic status or other problematic living circumstances. Your best ideas will come from learning about the needs of your community, such as these:

- Physical fitness
- Physical activity and active living to improve strength, cardiorespiratory health, and flexibility
- Good nutrition
- Achieving and maintaining a healthy weight
- Health education
- Smoking cessation
- Early detection, prevention, and treatment of illnesses such as diabetes, heart disease, and cancer
- Leisure education
- Reducing or treating substance abuse
- Stress management and time management
- Tutoring and mentoring with a health and physical activity focus
- After-school recreation activities
- Conducting program evaluations and writing grant proposals
- Improving social skills for improved peer and adult interactions
- Life skills and character development
- Sports, intramural activities, and other recreational pursuits
- Creative leisure pursuits such as arts and crafts, theater, and dance
- Adventure activities, outdoor programs, and environmental education

Although your class may find the project-launching activities and team building to be somewhat tedious, remember that *all* successful projects require careful planning and thorough preparation. Your patience and commitment will be rewarded. You will learn valuable lessons, the benefits of which will last far into the future.

There are two scenarios for choosing a service-learning project. In the first, the students help select the project. In the second scenario, the teacher, because of time constraints, chooses the project before the start of the first class. Regardless of how the project is chosen, your class has important things to do. In cases where the teacher has made decisions about the project ahead of time, he or she will decide which step 1 exercises you should complete.

SELECTING AND GETTING TO KNOW THE AGENCY

During the process of choosing a project, expect to visit and learn about more than one agency. If your teacher has already chosen the project, you will need to familiarize yourself with both your project and your agency.

Get Acquainted With the Learning Objectives

From the start of the project, you'll need to understand how the service-learning project will facilitate your learning. This will help you later when it is time to choose specific project tasks. Perhaps more important, it will help you maximize your learning during the reflection activities. Although your teacher could simply tell you why the project is worthwhile, you need to decide for yourself why the project is meaningful to you. In this short exercise, you will restate the class' learning goals and objectives into your own words. By doing so, you'll clarify what the project is about and why your class is doing it. (Note that you will revisit these goals and learning objectives—and you will develop them further—during the planning stage in step 3.)

Before you begin, learn the differences between goals and learning outcomes. Goals are general statements that are abstract and broadly stated. They are not specific and measurable. Learning outcomes are more precise and concrete. They state, in measurable terms, what students should be able to do by the end of the course (Huba and Freed 2000). Many classes have just one goal (such as the course description); others will have several goals, but there are typically several learning outcomes that specifically describe what knowledge, skills, and abilities students are expected to have by the end of the course.

Before you start rewriting the learning goals and outcomes, ask your teacher what the goals and learning outcomes are for your class, and determine which ones are directly related to the service-learning project. This information may be located on a class syllabus or course outline. To see how the process of rewriting works, consider the following example of a goal for college students who are majoring in physical education:

> Students will learn how to design and deliver a program that will increase the physical activity levels of elementary school–age children.

The service-learning students then write a complementary goal:

> Our class wants to design and deliver physical education programs in which we help younger children learn how to increase their levels of healthy physical activity.

After you write down your goal, compose some specific learning outcomes that relate to the goal. Remember, learning outcomes are the more detailed descriptions of the general ideas in the goals. Learning outcomes should be measurable and specific (see table 3.1 in step 3 for examples). The following are learning outcomes that would fit with the goals listed earlier:

- Students will be able to accurately assess the types and amount of physical activity the students do now.
- Students will be able to determine the kinds of physical activity that the students would like to learn more about and then take part in.
- Students will be able to compile a list of community resources that are already available to students who want to engage in physical activity.
- Students will be able to plan lessons and activities that are oriented toward healthy physical activity.
- Students will be able to deliver the lessons and conduct the activities.
- Students will be able to assist clients with setting goals and with maintaining their desired level of physical activity.

PhotoDisc

Writing preliminary goals and learning outcomes will help you and your team frame the project.

You don't need to spend a lot of time refining these statements at this point since this is a preliminary exercise that will help you and your classmates frame the project. Repeat this process for each class goal that relates to your service-learning project.

Here is something to keep in mind as you move ahead: You are looking for a great fit between the needs, abilities, and resources of your class and those of the agency. This type of win–win situation is the essence of good partnerships. Plenty of agencies need volunteers, but not many have suitable service-learning sites for your class. So keep these learning outcomes, and the qualities of a good service-learning project, in mind as you forge ahead. You are now ready to determine the scope of your project.

Describe What Your Team Can Do

It is time for you and your classmates to think about the scope of an ideal project and to define the range of tasks your class can perform. Since many agencies need a lot of help, it may be tempting to agree to a bigger project than you will have time, abilities, or resources to complete. Getting a clear picture of what your class can and cannot do will help you avoid committing to a task that requires more work than your class can reasonably do.

Your description needs to reflect what your class is able and willing to do. Be as accurate as possible in describing the skills, knowledge, support, and resources that you can bring to a project. The class and teacher should create a list of items that describe the scope of an ideal service-learning project. Even if the teacher has already chosen the project, it may be helpful to put this list together. For example, a description of the project by the college students who are majoring in physical education might say the following:

- Our physical education teacher preparation class at Your State University has 35 students who are training to become elementary school physical education teachers. We'll need plenty of tasks so that everyone can work directly with clients.
- We have experience in teaching children about physical activities, but we have not yet had a chance to deliver a comprehensive program for elementary students. The teacher will help us design a program, but she will not be with us at all times during the project. Therefore, our students will need some oversight and assistance from agency supervisors.
- We have physical activity and sports equipment that we can bring to the site. Therefore, the clients will not need to bring their own equipment.
- We want to start around February 1. The time frame for our project is January 15 through April 1.

Be as clear and as thorough as possible about what your class is willing and able to do in terms of learning objectives, time frames, resources, expertise, facilities, and so on. You can use your list in two ways: to evaluate whether your class should take on a particular project at a given agency, and to communicate to the agency partner what you are willing and able to do. You are now ready to find an appropriate service-learning project.

Locate Potential Partners

If your teacher has already chosen the project, he or she may have you skip this part as well as some of exercises that follow.

First, determine what resources are available for locating a suitable project. If your school has a service-learning center, the center will likely have information about potential agencies. Networking with students, teachers, and parents can also yield good ideas. You can contact schools, senior centers and nursing homes, churches, homeless shelters, police departments, juvenile justice programs, or other social services agencies in the area to locate potential partners who have needs that fit with your class' interests and abilities.

Brainstorm a list of locations in your area where people might need your class's services. (A detailed approach to brainstorming is discussed in step 2, page 29.) You may want to begin with the examples of direct service ideas at the start of this chapter. In addition, consult the phone book, newspapers, and the Internet. Review your list, narrow it down, and obtain the contact information for the agencies that interest you. You are almost ready to call some potential agencies, but first consider what you will say during your first conversation.

Write an Introduction Before Making Calls

Before you write your introduction, consider two possible approaches. Each approach has its advantages and disadvantages. You might even decide to combine the two approaches, using the best parts of each.

The first approach focuses on agency needs. Start by contacting promising agencies to find out what their clients need, and tailor your introduction to their needs. Write a general statement that will allow an agency's employee to tell you, in general, about the agency's needs. If the connection seems promising, you can use what you have learned about their clients' needs to design a service-learning project that directly meets those needs.

This approach makes it easier to find receptive clients because you've asked them what they need and you've designed a service to meet those needs. The downside is that the client's needs may not be well suited to your class' knowledge, skills, abilities, or learning objectives. The following is an example for college juniors in a recreation programming class:

> Our recreation programming class is looking for a service-learning project. Do students at your school have any need for recreation programming, such as team building or recreational sports? Who can we contact to find out more information?

You would then follow up to get more information about the students and to discuss how and when the programs might be conducted.

The second approach focuses on class needs. Start by writing a more specific description of the type of service-learning project your class would like to conduct, and then start looking for an agency whose clients need those services. With this approach you get more input from the potential client. The downside is that it might be more difficult to find a client with needs that match what you want to do. Here is an example of an introduction:

> Our recreation programming class at YSU is looking for a service-learning project. We are learning the basics of recreation programming. We would like to work directly with young people to help them learn more about getting along with others through healthy recreational activities. We would start by meeting the children and their teachers to find out more about the issues they are facing. We would then design team-building and recreational sports activities to meet their needs. At the end of the program, we would do a short evaluation to determine the effects of the program. Our instructor will help us design and implement this program.

If your class chooses to combine these two approaches, you could have a phone conversation that focuses on the client's needs, and you could provide examples of what your class has in mind. If an agency does *not* have specific ideas about its clients' needs, you will be prepared with a specific outline. Congratulations! You are now ready to contact potential agency partners.

Andreas Polk/Taxi/Getty Images

Phone calls to prospective agencies are a vital part of the planning process.

Make Initial Agency Inquiries

Make brief phone calls to the agencies on your list in order to determine whether their clients have needs that match your proposed services. Introduce yourself using the introduction you have prepared. If the response is positive, use your prepared questions to gather more information. Consider the following examples of follow-up questions:

- Do your clients (or students, or whatever term fits) have an interest in or need for this type of program?
- How many clients would likely be involved?
- Has another group ever conducted a service-learning project at your school?
- If we were to do a service-learning project at your school, would we be able to work directly with the clients?
- How much time will your staff have to collaborate with us on this project?
- Are you interested in meeting with us to further explore the possibility of a partnership?

Keep a log of your phone calls. Also keep the names of your contacts and notes from the conversations. Once you have collected this basic information from several agencies, your class can evaluate the possible project sites.

Review and Evaluate

As a group, review the information your team has gathered and evaluate the potential agencies. Consider each of the following criteria, which are qualities of good service-learning experiences:

- Do the clients' needs and interests appear to be genuine?
- Will the students be excited about the project?
- Will students have an opportunity to help others through direct service, and are there enough tasks to allow everyone to do meaningful work?
- Will the service be challenging, meaningful, and necessary?
- Is the agency willing and able to be an active partner, or will they want you to run the project on your own?
- Is there a good fit between your learning goals and the needs of the agency and its clients?

At this point, you will probably want to narrow your list down to the two or three most promising sites. Your next step is to visit the sites.

Make Initial Visits

As stated earlier, communication is the key to all successful partnerships. Assume nothing about an agency. Therefore, face-to-face communication is essential at this point because what you've learned over the telephone may be different from what you find when you visit an agency.

Visit the sites when the people you need to meet will be able to spend time with the students and the teacher. At that time the students can see the site firsthand and meet some of the clients. Don't overwhelm the agency with visitors. Check ahead of time to see how many students should visit. Check to see whether students may speak informally with clients. During this initial visit, you will share information, ask questions, and make general observations.

Information to Share

- Share information about your team, such as the number of students, the ages of the students, the type of class, the class' learning goals, and the time frame for your project.
- Review what you've learned about the agency's needs. For instance, you might say, "During our phone conversation, you said that the children in the after-school program don't have enough opportunities to be physically active. You also mentioned that cliques are forming within the group and that kids sometimes pick fights with each other. Is this accurate? Can you add anything else that might help us design a good program?"

Questions to Ask

- Do you think there is a good fit between what our class wants to do and what you need?
- What kind of tasks would you like us to perform?
- Do you think there will be enough tasks to allow all the students to do meaningful work?
- Will we have enough time to get to know the people we will work with before we start?

- How involved would you like to be in our planning process?
- What is your timeline for this project?

Observations to Make

- Did the staff members seem rushed, or did they make time to talk with you during our visit? The best predictor of future behavior is past behavior, so the way they treat you now is an indicator of how they will treat you in the future.
- Are the clients excited about you working with them? Did they express enthusiasm for what you are offering to do?
- Is the site safe? Are there foreseeable dangers? If there are, can precautions be taken? Here is a point for your teacher to consider: Will the school's administrators agree to having students work at the site?

Your class is now ready to choose an agency for your service-learning project. Ideally, your class will have visited two or three sites. Gather everyone to compare notes and to decide which project is best for you. If you need assistance with decision making, refer to the exercise on problem solving and decision making in step 2.

RETURN VISITS TO THE SITE AND CONTRACTING

Now that you have selected an agency and a project, your next action is to visit the agency and its clients at least two more times in order to gather more information and build relationships. We call this process of *contracting*, because you'll make a formal agreement with the agency about what your class will do and what you expect from them. This type of formal agreement is invaluable because it clarifies what partners can expect from each other. Once you complete your return visits and finish your contracting, you will have accomplished the launching of your service-learning project.

We'll review the characteristics of successful projects now so that you understand what you are trying to accomplish. During the return visits, you'll ensure that your class and the agency partner do the following:

- Commit to a common vision.
- Understand how your learning objectives are compatible with the service you'll be performing.
- Know each other's agendas and needs so that each party feels that it is compatible with the other.
- Know about each other's styles and limitations.
- Communicate frequently and openly about goals, tasks, roles, and accountability.

First Return Visit

Plan for your first return visit by reviewing the following discussion, which describes how to learn about client needs, how to share your needs, and how to gather information for project planning. During this visit, you will learn more

Corporation for National and Community Service

Site visits are opportunities to gather information and build relationships.

about the agency, and you will share details about your service-learning project. Before you return to the agency, discuss what to wear and how to behave. Also decide who will ask the questions—teachers, students, or a combination thereof (see sidebar titled Showing Professionalism in step 2, page 32). Have someone take notes.

It is possible to find out midway through the contracting that your class and the agency are not as good of a partner fit as you had thought. The discussion of contracting that follows will help you decide whether to continue with the contracting process. If you decide to not continue with the current agency and to start again, continue using this process until you find a good partner fit.

Assess Clients' Needs

Assessing clients' needs is like preparing the soil in a garden: Good, loose soil will produce beautiful plants, while untilled soil with clay and rocks will yield little. Use the following guidelines to prepare questions for your visit.

Your goal is to ensure that the service you plan to deliver will be meaningful to, and desired by, the clients.

- As a class, discuss the details of the service you plan to deliver. Ask yourselves whether the clients and staff appear to be excited about your project.
- Ask the agency staff and clients, "If you could have our service project change or improve just one thing, what would it be?" Their answer will tell you what is important to them.

Your goal is to clarify the needs and agendas of the agency and clients.

- Ask the clients and staff, "What do you need from this service project? What do you most need us to do?"
- Ask, "Do you have any concerns or worries about what might happen during the project?"
- Ask, "Have you worked with students on service-learning projects in the past? What went well, and what could we improve on?"

In most cases, a formal needs assessment survey is not required. But if you are working on a long-term (year or more) project, or if conducting a needs assessments is one of your learning outcomes, you may want to do one. If you believe that a more detailed needs assessment is in order, refer to appendix A: Designing Needs Assessments and Evaluations.

Share Information

In addition to gathering information about clients' needs, you'll want to share information about your class' needs with the agency staff and clients. You can use the following suggestions to determine what information to share with agency staff and clients.

Your goal is to determine how much direct contact the students will have with clients and whether there will be enough work to allow every student to do something meaningful.

- Find out how many clients can reasonably be expected to take part in the program.
- Find out how many roles there are for students to play. Will each of these roles involve direct interaction with clients? If not, will students be able to change roles during the project in order to give everyone a chance to work directly with clients?

Your goal is to make sure that the level of tasks is compatible with the students' knowledge, skills, and abilities. If it's not compatible, will you, the students, be able to get the support you need?

- Ask the agency staff whether students will need to work independently—if so, how much? When agencies are short staffed, they may not be able to provide much assistance to students during the service-learning project. If the students need assistance and if the agency can't provide it, you'll want to find out if the school can provide teachers or other staff to give you the support you need.

Your goal is to achieve your learning outcomes as you perform your service.

- Tell the agency staff about your project and about what you expect to do. You want the agency staff members to be comfortable with the students, with your level of expertise, and with your work. For example, if you plan to independently design and lead educational programs, you'll want to confirm, in advance, that the agency staff is comfortable with that.

- Service learning has many benefits beyond meeting your class' learning outcomes. Your project should also allow for leadership development, learning, sharing, and friendship. When you are able to provide meaningful service to others through your project, these benefits are more likely to occur.

Negotiate Details

This section asks you to consider some details that may seem insignificant now but that may become important later. These details can sometimes hinder a service-learning project. The following suggestions will help you determine whether the project will unfold in a way that is beneficial for everyone.

Your goal is to specify what the agency and clients will need from you and what you, the students, will need from them.

- Share information and ask questions about time frames (the start and end dates for the project), facilities, equipment, funding, and supervision. For example, if you need money for supplies, will you raise that money yourselves or will the agency help out? Does the agency feel comfortable with the time frame? What are the ideal start and end dates?
- As you determine whether the project is feasible given the available resources (time, money, people, expertise), remember that you can negotiate compromises and that you can seek outside support (such as small grants or donations) if more resources are needed. The point is to resolve potential problems now rather than later.

Your goal is to find out about other details you should consider before making a final commitment to the project.

- Ask the agency whether you need any volunteer paperwork, insurance, medical checks, special training, or background checks. These are concerns in certain clinical settings.
- If there are special needs, find out if the agency or your school can help with any of them.

Your goal is to make the agency's staff aware of the commitments your class is asking them to make to the service-learning project.

- Ask the agency's staff members whether they are willing and able to acquaint students with the site and the clients.

Corporation for National and Community Service

Detailed planning will help ensure that your project runs smoothly.

- Make sure that the staff members will be on site and available during the project if the students need supervision and assistance.
- Find out whether staff members are willing and able to participate in reflection, evaluation, and celebration activities at the end of the project.

Decide Whether to Continue

At this point you have gathered a lot of information. Remember that you are looking for a project in which the partners' agendas and needs are compatible. If you have concerns, make sure you discuss them with your teacher. If both the agency and the class are enthusiastic about the project and if there seems to be a good fit, then continue on. If either partner is uncertain about the project, then come up with a plan to make a decision (that is, who needs to decide what and by when). If you decide to not work with the agency, inform the agency promptly. Otherwise, set up your next visit with the agency after you've reviewed the follow-up items in the next section.

Follow Up

Now that you have chosen a project site, there are three more things to do.

1. Determine how and when to build personal relationships with your clients.
2. Restate what you've heard and formalize your commitment.
3. Set up a preliminary schedule.

You will need to visit the site again in order to build relationships. The timing of your visit depends on your project. It may be best to do it either before the official start date or on the official start date. Read through the following discussion and, with your teacher, determine how to take care of these final details. You can probably handle all of these items with phone calls and with one or more visits.

Build Personal Relationships With Your Clients

Before delivering a direct service, take time to build personal relationships with your clients. This is especially critical if your clients come from a background that is different from yours. Deep down, people have more in common than they have differences, but differences are what people see first. Diversity can be an asset to your service-learning experience, but differences can turn into barriers if you don't first discover what you have in common.

Ask the agency's staff members and your teacher the following questions:

- How can we truly get to know our clients as people?
- Do you think some introductory sessions or activities would be helpful? [Present the agency with the activity ideas in appendix B, which contains several excellent diversity-awareness icebreaker activities that can be used as starting points. If these activities are not appropriate, see if your teacher, school guidance counselor, or agency staff members have suggestions. Find out who would be willing to facilitate some meetings for you. If you decide to use these activities, decide who will facilitate them. Possible facilitators are students, school counselors, agency staff, or your teacher.]
- Would you like to schedule some time for some relationship-building activities with the clients and the students? (When appropriate, schedule time to do some or all of the diversity-awareness icebreaker activities with your clients as you complete step 2 and begin the planning process in step 3.)

Also consider asking the agency's staff members some of these specific questions about your clients:

- What can you tell us about your clients' lives and needs? What concerns do they have that you think our project might be able to help with?
- How do you think they will respond to having students around?
- What else can you suggest to help us get to know them better?

Restate What You've Heard and Formalize Your Commitment

Use active-listening principles by restating what the team is committing to do and what you believe the agency is committing to do. (A detailed discussion of good listening is included in step 2, page

19.) After you've reached a verbal agreement with the agency, we recommend that you formalize your commitment in writing.

Thank the agency staff members for their time. Restate your understanding of what the agency and clients need and what services the students can provide. Also restate what each group (the agency and the students) is committing to. Here is an example of what you might say: "Thank you for taking time to meet with us today. I would like to restate my understanding of our roles in this service-learning project so that I can make sure we all understand everything correctly." Make sure the conversation continues until there is an agreement on everything. Don't forget to make sure that someone is taking notes! We recommend preparing a formal, written agreement to send to the agency.

Next write a confirmation letter to the agency. In this letter, restate what was agreed to, and provide details about the service-learning project. At a minimum, include the following:

- A description of the project
- A list of what your class will do and what the agency has agreed to do
- A timeline for the project; include key dates and times for events
- A thank-you note to the agency for agreeing to work with your class on the project

A sample letter is shown in figure 1.1.

In addition to making formal contact with the agency that you intend to partner with, make sure to contact any agencies you've spoken with but did not choose. Thank them for their time, and let them know that your class has chosen a different site for your service-learning project. If you think a future class might like to work with the agency, provide the agency with a contact from your school.

Set Up a Preliminary Schedule

Before you leave the meeting, arrange a date for the students to begin working with clients. Recognize that your team will need time to learn class content and to prepare for the service-learning project. The class will do this preparation during step 2, so look ahead and estimate how much planning time will be needed. This preliminary timeline should also include any other issues that need to be resolved before the project begins:

- The completion of any paperwork required by the agency
- Required medical checks

Dear School Social Worker and After-School Program Staff:

It has been our pleasure to meet you and the students and to discuss the details of our service-learning project. We plan to start the project on February 1 and to continue through the end of our school year on May 15. The students in our recreation programming class will arrive at the school every Monday through Thursday around 3:00 p.m. to help the students with homework and to conduct recreational activities during the after-school program. We will leave each day at 5:00 p.m.

Our school will provide transportation, recreation equipment, and volunteer insurance coverage. All students will have been informed that when they arrive at the school, they must first go to the school's office to sign in and to receive a name badge. We will bring a graduate assistant with us each day to serve in whatever capacity is needed that day. While we won't need help with leading the recreation activities, we do appreciate your offer to assist us with any behavior-management problems that might arise.

Thank your for agreeing to let us work with the students in your after-school program. We believe this will be a valuable learning experience for everyone, and we are excited about the orientation you have planned for us on February 1.

Sincerely,

The class and the teacher

Figure 1.1 Sample confirmation letter.

- Orientation to computers or to other specialized equipment
- Facility and equipment orientation, specialized training (such as CPR and first aid), and so on

Those, of course, are just examples. You should work directly with your teacher to resolve questions specific to your project.

REFLECTION

Reflecting on a regular basis will help you get the most out of your service-learning project. Gail Albert, a service-learning educator with the Vermont Commission on National and Community Service, has several good ideas for starting the reflection process. Albert advocates setting the context for reflection by writing down your preconceptions and expectations before you start the project. Otherwise, by the time you finish the project, you may not remember how you felt at the beginning. One creative way to do this is to write a letter to yourself, seal it, and leave it with the teacher. At the end of the project, the teacher returns your letter for you to reread. You can then reflect verbally or in writing on what you've learned and on how your views have changed.

Another way to facilitate reflection is to set aside 5 to 10 minutes during every group meeting for students to share their experiences and reflections. One way to facilitate this discussion is to follow a "what, so what, now what" format. Ask students to share their thoughts on what is going well and what is causing them concern. Follow with a question asking them how they feel about those events. To conclude, ask the group if anything should be done to follow up on any of these issues. It is probable that many of the students' thoughts and feelings will not need to be followed up, but it is also probable that some will.

Keeping a journal is another way for you to record your thoughts, feelings, and ideas. It is the most common method of reflection used in service learning. The following are various formats for keeping a journal. Your teacher will likely ask you to use one (or more) formats throughout the project.

Journal Formats

It's a good idea to decide as a class which format you all should use for keeping a journal. At the end of the project, each student will reflect on the project as a whole, and your journal entries will serve as building blocks. The Campus Compact recommends four journal formats for service-learning students to consider (Rama and Battistoni 2001):

1. **Unstructured journal.** Use a free-form journal format to record thoughts, feelings, observations, activities, and questions. Start writing in a journal early on in the project, and make frequent entries. Your teacher should review your entries and provide feedback. The benefits of keeping a journal include improving your observational skills, exploring your feelings, recording your progress, and improving your communication. If you decide to use this type of journal format, decide how often you will make entries and when you will turn them in to the teacher.

2. **Structured journal.** A teacher may ask you to keep a structured journal in order to direct your attention to issues and questions that will connect the service project to the class objectives. The structure can range from reporting your feelings to completing problem-solving activities. Your teacher might ask you a question each week that will help you connect your experience to the class objectives. Or you could follow a cognitive-processing format—for instance, by responding to the following three questions: What happened? (Describe what happened to you, to others, to the clients). So what? (Describe what effect those events had on you and others. What did you observe that led you to believe this?). Now what? (Based on questions 1 and 2, how can you use this knowledge in the future?)

3. **Team journal.** You and the rest of the class can take turns recording shared and individual experiences, reactions, observations, and responses to each other's entries. If you keep a team journal, consider setting up a schedule for who is responsible for writing in it and when. You may be asked to respond to structured questions such as "Who did I learn something from today?" or to subject-matter questions such as "What did today's experience teach you about program planning?" or "How does the concept of diversity relate to today's experience?" (Albert 1996). Also consider whether you want the journal to be a book, a butcher-paper run around the walls of the classroom, or an electronic journal, such as a blog.

4. **Critical-incidents journal**. In a critical-incidents journal you are asked to record a minimum of one critical incident for each week of the service project. The events could include solving a problem, making a decision, or handling a conflict. This type of journal format provides a forum for communicat-

ing problems and challenges, and it can facilitate open communication. As with the team journal, consider whether you want the critical-incidents journal to be in an electronic or paper format.

Adapted from Rama and Battistoni 2001. http://www.compact.org/disciplines/reflection/types.html

Tips for Journaling

Mark Cooper (n.d.), the author of "The big dummy's guide to service-learning," shares important tips for keeping a great journal.

- Journals should be snapshots filled with descriptions of sights, sounds, and smells, as well as with concerns, insights, doubts, fears, and critical questions about issues, other people, and, most important, yourself.
- Honesty is the most important ingredient for successful journals.
- A journal is not a work log of tasks, events, times, and dates.
- Write freely. Grammar and spelling should not be stressed until the final draft.
- Write an entry after each visit. If you can't write a full entry, jot down random thoughts and images, which you can return to a day or two later and expand into a colorful, verbal picture.
- Use journaling as a way to meditate on what you've seen, felt, and experienced, and on what continues to excite, trouble, impress, or unnerve you.
- Don't simply answer questions in your journal. Also let your questions spur you to think of more questions. Use the questions to focus your writing. Refer to the section Final Journals in step 5 for samples of questions that you can write about in your day-to-day journals and in your final reflection journals.

Based on M. Cooper, *The big dummy's guide to service-learning: 27 simple answers to good questions on: Faculty, programmatic, student, administration & non-profit issues.* Available: http://www.fiu.edu/~time4chg/Library/reflect.html.

SUMMARY

Launching your service-learning project requires communication and an attention to detail. Give yourselves a pat on the back for what you've accomplished. During this process, I hope you have discovered that you are needed in your community and that you need to prepare a solid foundation for your project. The best is yet to come. By completing the exercises in this chapter, you have benefited from the collective wisdom of the many teachers and students who have gone before you.

REFERENCES

Albert, G. 1996. Intensive service-learning experiences. In B. Jacoby (Ed.), *Service-learning in higher education.* San Francisco: Jossey-Bass.

Andres, S. 1993. Working together for youth: A practical guide for individuals and groups. www.servicelearning.org/library/lib_cat/index.php?action=detailed&item=1552.

Cooper, M. n.d. The big dummy's guide to service-learning. www.fiu.edu/~time4chg/Library/bigdummy.html.

Huba, M.E., and J.E. Freed. 2000. *Learner-centered assessment of college campuses: Shifting the focus from teaching to learning.* Needham Heights, MA: Allyn & Bacon.

Kurt Hahn Quotes. n.d. In *Wilderdom's* Web site. www.wilderdom.com/Hahn.htm.

Learn and Serve America Clearinghouse. n.d. Building effective partnerships in service-learning. Fact sheet. www.servicelearning.org/instant_info/fact_sheets/cb_facts/build_partners/index.php.

Rama, D.V., and R. Battistoni. 2001. Service-learning: Using structured reflection to enhance learning from service. www.compact.org/disciplines/reflection/index.html.

Sugerman, D.A., K.L. Doherty, D.E. Garvey, and M.A. Gass. 2000. *Reflective learning: Theory and practice.* Dubuque, IA: Kendall/Hunt.

REFLECTION

In addition to the journaling assigned by your teacher, a reflection activity that may be useful is called Hopes and Fears in a Hat (Sugerman, Doherty, Garvey, and Gass 2000). This activity takes 20 to 40 minutes depending on the size of your group. You'll need a hat. Give everyone in the group two pieces of paper. Have them write one hope and one fear they have about the service-learning project. Do not have the students write their names on the papers. Mix up the pieces of paper in the hat and have each student draw two pieces out of the hat. If someone picks his own paper, he should not say anything. No one will know. The students read the comments out loud. Have an open discussion about everyone's hopes and fears. Group members will come to understand that many others share their feelings. Continue this process until all the papers are read. Your class can revisit this reflection activity at any point if the students seem to be anxious about the project.

STUDENT CHECKLIST

- ☐ The selected project is a good fit with the class's learning objectives—learning will take place.
- ☐ Both the students and the clients are excited about the project.
- ☐ There will be enough challenging, valuable, and necessary work for everyone to do.
- ☐ The goals and objectives for the project are written down, and the students, teacher, and agency all agree with them.
- ☐ It is feasible to complete the project in the time allotted and with the resources available.
- ☐ The site is safe, and arrangements have been made for completing any paperwork, medical checks, insurance forms, or background checks that are necessary for working with these clients.
- ☐ Arrangements have been made for the students to get to know the clients and the facilities.
- ☐ A confirmation letter has been sent to the clients for the service project you selected.
- ☐ Written or spoken contact has been made with the agencies you did not choose for your project.
- ☐ The students and teacher will use journals or other exercises to facilitate reflection throughout the project.

STEP

2

Building an Effective Team

Step 5
Finishing the Project

Step 4
Implementing the Plan

Step 3
Planning the Project

Step 2
Building an Effective Team

Step 1
Launching the Project

In this step you will

- **practice communication skills,**
- **develop group-process skills, such as brain-storming and problem solving, and**
- **learn team development and leadership styles.**

> **Coming together is a beginning. Keeping together is progress. Working together is success.**
>
> *—Henry Ford*

Teamwork happens when individuals work together to accomplish more than they could through their individual efforts. Typically, one plus one equals two; but when individuals form a team, one plus one becomes greater than two. High-functioning teams communicate effectively, work well together as a group, and understand the principles of team development. Perhaps you have learned teamwork skills in other classes. It makes sense to review and reinforce them before you begin your project. Good teams have fewer frustrations and waste less time than other teams.

Team skills are the foundation for your class' success with the service project. You will also discover that good teamwork and leadership skills are important in the future, both at work and away from work.

Your team will likely be working on step 2 at the same that you are working on steps 1 and 3. The information and activities in this section describe strategies for team building as well as solutions to stumbling blocks. If your group, at any point during your service-learning experience, needs to improve communication, conduct a meeting, brainstorm, or solve a problem, skip to the corresponding section in the text. The checklist at the end of this chapter can help you decide which team-building exercises will help solve the problems your team is encountering.

DEVELOPING EFFECTIVE COMMUNICATION SKILLS

According to Edward Wertheim, a business professor at Northeastern University, people in organizations spend more than 75 percent of their time involved in some kind of interpersonal situation. Therefore, it should come as no surprise that poor communications are at the root of most organizational problems (Wertheim n.d.). Effective communication is essential whether the communication is with the students, the teacher, the agencies, or the clients. When all team members learn basic communication skills, your project will be easier and more enjoyable. In this section you will learn skills for *assertive communication*, including establishing rapport, using "I" statements, listening, and providing constructive feedback. Each of these sections describes how to put the communication skills into practice. At the end, there is a role-play activity that will allow you to practice the skills.

Establishing Rapport

The first step to communicating effectively is to establish rapport. *Rapport* refers to a relationship based on mutal appreciation, on trust, and on a sense that the individuals understand and share each other's concerns. Good rapport is a key to success because it involves appreciating and working with differences (Ready and Burton 2004). When you establish good rapport with others, you make it easier to get things done, to provide good client service, and to save time and energy (Ready and Burton 2004). In short, when you have good rapport, you feel good about working with others.

Here are some communication techniques you can use to set a positive tone.

- Use the person's name.
- Smile and look directly in the person's eyes without getting in his personal space.
- Stand or sit up straight; don't slouch or lean, which gives the appearance of indifference.
- Begin the conversation with some small talk such as, "How was your morning?" Be prepared to truly listen to her answer, and do not respond with a superficial comment.
- Use the appropriate tone for the conversation. For example, when talking to a fellow student, use language and tone that are similar to his. When talking to a person in authority, such as a teacher or client supervisor, show appropriate respect.

A fun activity for learning people's names is the Ball-Toss Name Game. To play, obtain three to five balls that are soft, easy to throw, and easy to catch. Rubber balls work well. Have your group stand in a circle and tell them the guidelines for the game. Here is a sample script.

> The purpose of this game is for everyone to learn everyone else's first name. We will throw and catch balls while saying each other's names because this action helps people remember better. To begin, let's establish a ground rule that it's okay to forget someone else's name—all you have to do is ask. Learning names is difficult, so we should all give each other permission to ask each other's names as many times as we need to.
>
> Here's how the game works. We will go around the circle and each person will say his or her first name. Next I will call out someone's name and then throw her the ball. Note that I said, ". . . call her name first and *then* throw her the ball." It's not fair to call out a person's name while the ball is in the air. Once she catches the ball (or retrieves it in the event of a bad throw), she calls someone else's name and throws him the ball. The goal is to keep the ball moving as quickly as possible and to make sure that everyone is included. Once one ball gets going, I will introduce the other balls.

After the group seems to know each other's names, stop the game and collect the balls. Ask if anyone in the group thinks he can name everyone. End the game by reminding the players of the importance of using each other's names, and tell them again that it's best to ask someone's name if you forget.

Another activity you can use to establish rapport is called *partner drawings*. To do this activity, you'll need the following:

- Enough simple pictures for half your group (examples of pictures are trees, birds, houses, dogs, and clouds)
- Blindfolds for half your group
- Paper and pencils for half the group

Begin with the following introduction:

> We need to divide the group into pairs of two. If there is an odd number of students, one student will pair with the teacher. I will give each pair a piece of paper, a pencil, and a picture, which I will place facedown on the table. Choose one person to draw with the blindfold on; the other person will give directions. When you are ready, I will ask the person who is giving the directions to turn the picture over. That person then coaches his blind partner to draw her own version of the picture.

Afterward, ask the group to discuss what worked well and what didn't work well during the one-on-one time. Then, as a group, discuss what they learned about rapport, empathy, giving directions, listening, and giving feedback. During the discussion, look for examples of how rapport and empathy made a difference.

Here are some suggestions for putting rapport skills into practice.

- Before you begin a conversation, have a positive mental attitude. If your attitude is something less than positive, take some deep breaths and relax. Remind yourself that even when something seems wrong, communicating about it will likely resolve the problem. If you begin the conversation with a smile, a good attitude, and a relaxed posture, the conversation will probably go well.
- Commit to using a person's name whenever you speak to her. If you don't remember her name, just ask. If you then use her name right away, you will likely remember it.
- In addition to calling a person by name, remember to make a friendly inquiry such as, "How's your day going?" *Listen* to his answer.

In the sections that follow, you will work on improving your listening and feedback skills. These exercises will also help you establish rapport with your fellow students and with the teacher. Note that you can use these activities with your clients in addition to the icebreaker and diversity-awareness activities in appendix B.

Listening

When we meet someone new, many of us talk a lot about ourselves rather than listen to the other person. This is natural. We all want to be liked, and we believe that when others hear about us they will like us. But listening to people—not talking *at* them—causes them to see you in a positive light. Listening well is as powerful as speaking well.

Good listening, however, does not come naturally to most people. Listening well means paying attention to *how* you listen. Do you listen in a way that demonstrates understanding and respect? Figure 2.1 shows some listening practices to use and some to avoid. If you master these techniques, you will become a good listener. As your listening becomes more relaxed, you will become a listening artist.

Here are some suggestions for putting your listening skills into practice:

- Commit to listening to the other person before stating your ideas.
- Ask focused questions. This shows understanding, care, and concern. It also shows that you take the other person's ideas seriously.
- Avoid starting an important conversation when you are in a hurry. Find out what the person wants to talk about and say, "This is important, and I want to really hear what you have to say. Let's set up a time when we can talk about it." Then set a time and follow though.

Good listening requires a positive attitude. Respect is a critical element of listening well. This is especially true when you don't want to hear what someone else has to say. We've all been there! When this happens to you, remember to treat the person with the same respect you would hope for if the situation were reversed. Not everyone is right, but everyone deserves respect.

"I" Statements

"I" statements are a basic technique for becoming an assertive communicator. When we are unsure of what to say, we often use a passive approach, saying nothing. Or we use the opposite, aggressive approach, saying something that makes others feel attacked. The essence of effective assertive communication is expressing what you need and then asking for it in a constructive way. We need to learn how to communicate assertively in all situations, even when someone makes us feel uncomfortable.

The secret to assertive communication is to state *your* point of view rather than to assume that

Do:

- Prove that you care about what the person is saying by stopping everything else you are doing.
- Maintain good eye contact and relax your face.
- Listen for main ideas more than you listen for facts (McNamara n.d.).
- Prove that you understand a person's comments by occasionally restating part of his or her idea or by asking a thoughtful question. Saying "I understand" is not enough because it doesn't show that you really do understand (PAR Group 2007).
- Show respect for other people by taking their views seriously. It seldom helps to say to someone, "I know how you feel," because the comment will seem fake. You show respect by speaking with understanding. This means adjusting the words you use and changing your tone of voice, as well as varying your rate of speech and your choice of words (PAR Group 2007).

Don't:

- Use superficial phrases such as "I know how you feel" and "I understand."
- Remain expressionless. Don't slouch, look down, or fold your arms across your chest.
- Crowd the person's space, smoke, eat, or chew gum.
- Sigh or look at your watch while the person is speaking.
- Speak with an annoyed, impatient, or condescending tone of voice or words.
- Judge what the person is saying until he or she finishes (McNamara n.d.).

Figure 2.1 The dos and don'ts of good listening.

you know someone else's point of view. You can do this by using the "I" statement, a clear statement about how a situation or person made you feel. The statement is not so much polite (although it obviously should not be rude) as it is clear and assertive. It is neither passive nor aggressive.

"I" statements are so named because they always start with the word *I* instead of with the word *you*. For example, you can say, "I feel frustrated," instead of "You make me angry." Your understanding of the situation or of the other person's actions may or may not be valid, but your feelings are valid, and you own them through the "I" statement. The "I" statement opens the door to a constructive discussion, because when others know how you feel, it is easier to engage in nondefensive, clear communication.

One way to begin is with the phrase "The way I see it . . . " An even better phrase is "When you . . . I feel" formula. Here is an example: "When you arrive late for meetings, I feel frustrated and angry." Ideally, you and the other person will then discuss and resolve the issue without hurting each other's feelings.

When you know something needs to be said but you're not sure where to begin, stop and think before you speak. Also consider the following:

- Recall the starter words "When you . . . " and "I feel . . . ."
- Describe the person's behavior using nonjudgmental language. Give only descriptive facts so that the person knows exactly what you are talking about.
- Remember that the feelings are yours and that feelings are not facts—they are just feelings.

If you fill in the information that is relevant to your situation, you will be on your way to becoming an assertive communicator. If you begin a conversation in this descriptive way, while owning your feelings, the conversation will probably turn out well.

Constructive Feedback

The term *constructive feedback* is often used interchangeably with *criticism*, but there is a subtle difference. When you give constructive feedback, your attitude is kind and helpful. But when you criticize, your attitude may be less kind and more judgmental. Even when the feedback is constructive, however, many people are so sensitive that any correction is perceived as a personal attack. Therefore, they may become defensive.

Any time you work with others, constructive feedback is necessary. Your team can do two things to facilitate communication. First, make it clear in your ground rules (discussed in greater detail on page 30) that constructive feedback is needed and valued. Second, study the information in this chapter so that you can learn how to give constructive feedback.

Motivation experts Jennifer La Guardia and Richard Ryan (2002) note that people are discouraged by demeaning criticism. This negative feeling, which we've all experienced, is a big reason why some people are reluctant to give critical feedback. They're afraid that people will be offended or that they will become angry. A lesson that many of us were taught as children is "If you don't have something nice to say, don't say anything." Second, because we know that many people take criticism personally and that they become defensive, many people are afraid to give even the most constructive feedback. But constructive feedback, delivered in a caring manner, is not personal. To give constructive feedback, first establish rapport with the person you're talking to so that she will know that you like and accept her. It will be easier for her to understand that you are simply responding to a situation that you believe needs attention.

Here are a couple of guidelines that you will follow during the Practicing Good Communication Skills activity. First, deliver feedback as soon as possible after the precipitating event. The most useful feedback (whether positive or constructive) happens right as something occurs. Of course, you should respect a person's privacy; you may therefore need to give your feedback later in a one-on-one situation, but do it as soon as possible.

Second, apply the simple DASR (describe, acknowledge, specify, and reaffirm) formula described by Patti Hathaway, "the Change Agent" (1990).

Describe the exact behavior you find troublesome. Be specific and do not exaggerate. Just describe what happened or what was said.

Acknowledge how you feel about the other person's behavior or about the situation. Use "I" statements.

Specify what needs to happen. Present clear information, including actions and deadlines when relevant.

Reaffirm that you like the person, and express confidence in his ability to correct the situation.

Based on P. Hathaway, 1990, Giving and receiving criticism, *The Change Agent* pg. 44.

The DASR method can be used any time you need to speak to someone about his performance. For example, perhaps a classmate agreed to get you some information by a certain time but he didn't follow through and he didn't call to explain why. Another example is that you observe a classmate interacting with a client in a demeaning way, such as by speaking to an elderly nursing-home resident as though that resident were a child. In both of these examples, you would have legitimate thoughts to share, but in order for the classmate to hear the message without becoming defensive, you will need to be careful of what you say and how you say it.

Table 2.1 compares less effective and more effective ways of using the DASR method.

Learning how to give constructive feedback is a challenge, but receiving someone else's critique is also difficult. Even though constructive feedback is indispensable to a functioning team, most people find that even the most constructive criticism is difficult to hear without becoming defensive. Hathaway (1990) has some tips that can help you view constructive feedback as a gift, or as an opportunity to grow, rather than as a threat:

- Try to remember that a critique is not the same as disapproval. Constructive criticism provides an opportunity for personal growth. It is good that we care enough about each other to tell someone when something is bothering us.
- When someone critiques you, try to avoid the two most common responses: counterattacking (the defensive approach) and saying nothing (the passive approach). Instead tell yourself, "This is just a critique. It's not personal." You can then assess the merit of the person's comments.
- Listen intently and ask for more information if you don't understand. Then assess whether the feedback is valid. Consider this:
  - Have you heard the same thing from others?
  - Does the critic know about this subject?
  - Is the critic usually a fair and reasonable person?
  - Is the critique about me, or is the person just having a bad day?
  - Is this an issue that I need to respond to?
- If you decide that the feedback is valid and important, take action. If you decide that it is invalid or not important, you may choose to grin and bear it, ignore it (but be careful about giving away your true feelings if you are offended), or disagree politely.

Giving and receiving constructive feedback are two of the most important and challenging communication skills you can learn. If you find that they do not come naturally to you, take small steps

Table 2.1 Using the DASR Method

	Less effective	More effective
Describe	"You always interrupt me."	"When you interrupt me while I'm speaking . . . "
Acknowledge	"You make me so angry I could just walk out of class and never come back."	"I feel like you are not listening to what I have to say. I get frustrated because my ideas are not heard, and I think I have some good ones."
Specify	"Can't you wait until I'm finished talking before you jump in?"	"I'd appreciate it if you could wait until I'm finished talking before you start talking."
Reaffirm	"It will work better that way."	"I appreciate that you have a lot of energy for the project, and I know we can work together to make sure that everyone's ideas are heard."

by consciously practicing the DASR formula until you are comfortable. Practice makes perfect, and your service-learning project provides an ideal environment for learning and developing these skills. Try to have fun with the process. You'll know that the class is growing when people are having fun with it and are even jokingly giving feedback on the feedback.

Giving Compliments

As important as constructive criticism is, offering positive feedback is just as meaningful. Noticing what people do well and then giving them compliments will foster a positive, friendly atmosphere among your team. It has been said that it takes four compliments to outweigh one critique and to thereby bolster a person's sense of self-worth (Mitchell and Meier 1983). Even a poorly delivered compliment is better than none at all. But positive feedback is most effective when it is specific and immediate. A generic compliment such as "Good job" is a start, but compliments should contain enough information to allow the student to understand exactly what she did well. This will help her repeat the action in the future.

You can use part of the DASR formula to deliver effective compliments:

Describe the exact action that was good. Use "When you . . . " as a starting point, and then describe what he did. For example, "When you brought all those completed posters today, I was really happy to see them."

Acknowledge that what he did was good, and describe how his action was a benefit to either the team, the client, the teacher, or even the person himself. For example, "They look so great! I'm sure they'll help us recruit plenty of volunteers."

The most important things to remember about compliments are to catch people doing things right and to let them know right away that you appreciate what they did. To practice giving compliments, commit to complimenting others as often as possible. Set a goal to give a certain number of compliments per day. Start with one and increase by one a day to two, three, four, or more. Remember, practice makes perfect, and giving genuine compliments is a great way to brighten your day and the day of everyone around you. You'll feel good because you are focusing on the positive, and they'll feel good because you noticed.

In the following activity, you will use the DASR method to practice listening and to give critical feedback and compliments. These communication skills will feel a little artificial because you will not be given enough context to know how you would respond in real life. The DASR works so well, however, that it will increase your confidence in how to use assertive communication skills in real life. It is important to do this activity with a light and playful attitude. It should never be graded.

Practicing Communication Skills

Three scenarios are presented here (your teacher may want to write one or more scenarios that are more specific to your class's situation). Divide yourselves into groups of three students, each of whom will act out the scenarios (use one or more groups of four if the numbers divide evenly). Each person will take a turn in each of the three roles: speaker, listener, and observer. The speaker tries to use guidelines for good communication in describing the scenario to the listener. The listener should act normal and try not to make the situation too easy or too difficult for the speaker. After the acting out of each scenario, the observer writes about what the speaker did well, did only a little bit, or did not do at all during each role play. Remember, this is a learning exercise, so make honest observations. It will be helpful if you write brief comments as you observe.

After each student completes the role play, give that person a chance to talk about what he thinks he did well and how he could have improved. When the speaker is finished with his self-evaluation, the observer should give her feedback and show the speaker the checklist.

➤ *Listening*

Speaker: Your class has elected you to be the student leader for your service-learning project. Everyone knew that yesterday's meeting was important because your group needed to decide who would do each job. You need to speak to a student who was not present at the meeting. Speak with her and listen carefully to your classmate's responses.

Listener: You missed an important class in which everyone decided which tasks they would perform during the service-learning project. You know you made a mistake in not telling anyone, and now you're embarrassed because you realized you should have called someone. You missed class because your cat was sick. You took her to the vet and several expensive tests need to be run. You're still worried about the situation.

LISTENING			
	Did not do	**Did a little**	**Did really well**
Established rapport • I used the person's name. • I smiled and was relaxed. • I talked to the person at her level. • I started with small talk, and I listened.			
Showed good understanding • I remarked on main ideas. • I asked good questions. • I acknowledged the other person's feelings.			
I avoided • poor eye contact, • looking disinterested, • superficial comments, • interrupting.			

➤ *Constructive Criticism*

Speaker: You are the student leader for a conference. A classmate agrees to shop for the refreshments for the class' meeting with your clients. A half hour before the event, he arrives without the refreshments.

Listener: You agreed to shop for the refreshments for your class's meeting with your clients. Your friend called last night, however, and was upset. You listened to her instead of doing the shopping. You show up a half hour before the event with no refreshments.

CONSTRUCTIVE CRITICISM			
	Did not do	**Did a little**	**Did really well**
Established rapport • I used the person's name. • I smiled and was relaxed. • I talked to the person at his level. • I started with small talk, and I listened.			
Described • I began with "When you . . . " • I described the specific behavior.			
Acknowledged • I began with "I feel . . . " • I explained how the person's action made me feel.			

CONSTRUCTIVE CRITICISM *(continued)*			
	Did not do	**Did a little**	**Did really well**
Specified • I explained what would be better. • I gave specific details.			
Reaffirmed • I expressed confidence and support for the listener.			
I avoided • using an accusing tone, • starting with "You . . ., " and • making comments that were too general.			

➤ *Compliments*

Speaker: You are planning children's activities with your classmate for the health fair. You've been busy with your other classes and have not had time to plan anything yet. Your classmate shows up with several library books that will make your task easy and fun.

Listener: You are planning children's activities with your classmate for the health fair. Last night you checked out several library books with excellent activities that will make your job easy and fun. You share these books with your classmate.

COMPLIMENTS			
	Did not do	**Did a little**	**Did really well**
Established rapport • I used the person's name. • I smiled and was relaxed. • I talked to the person at her level. • I started with small talk, and I listened.			
Described • I began with "When you . . . " • I gave specifics about what the person did well.			
Acknowledged • I described one benefit of the person's good act. • Benefits could be to the group, the teacher, the client, or the person herself.			
I avoided • comments that were too superficial or too general, and • appearing insincere.			

GROUP-PROCESS SKILLS

The term *group process* refers to how people behave in groups—for example, in groups that have a task to complete—as well as to how they solve problems and make decisions (Ready and Burton 2004). Group process requires good communication skills, such as the ones you've already learned. But for groups to become effective, they must also know how conduct meetings, brainstorm, solve problems, and make decisions.

It's also important for the group to establish ground rules. While the teacher could simply dictate rules to the class, it is best for the class to discuss and establish its own rules, with assistance from the teacher or other facilitator. When students help determine the ground rules, they feel a greater sense of ownership of the team. It is also more likely that everyone will feel a commitment to good group process.

The final component of group process is team development. When groups understand the process of team development, they know what to expect as they move through the process of becoming a high-functioning team.

Conducting Efficient Meetings

Throughout the process of planning your service-learning project, your team will have many meetings. A subject as simple as meetings may not seem worthy of special attention. Ineffective meetings, however, can result in wasted time, frustration, and stunted accomplishment. Your class time is limited and valuable. You owe it to yourselves to carefully review these simple yet essential guidelines for conducting meetings. Keep in mind that not every suggestion will apply to every meeting or class situation, but knowing the basics will help you stay on track. These meeting guidelines were adapted from the Free Management Library (1997-2008).

Assigning Roles

It's helpful to assign roles since it is very difficult for one person to manage all the elements of a successful meeting. These roles can be filled by students or by teachers. Key roles within a meeting include the following:

- The task leader calls and facilitates the meeting.
- The social leader creates a welcoming and comfortable atmosphere (which may entail such tasks as conducting icebreakers, supplying refreshments, and making the facility as comfortable as possible).
- The meeting manager helps keep the meeting on track and ensures that everyone follows the ground rules.
- The minutes taker records decisions and makes notes about what was agreed to.

Often, the teacher will start as the task leader in order to model the role for students. Later on, she can allow the students to take over. Your class may choose to have just one person fill each role for the duration of the project, or you can rotate people into each position so that more students can experience and share the workload. Students who are not assigned to specific roles will actively participate in the discussion in each meeting.

Planning the Meeting

The person convening the meeting—usually the teacher or designated task leader—determines the purpose of the meeting. Purposes can include planning, sharing information, problem solving, training, and debriefing. The meeting's purpose determines who should be involved.

The person in charge of planning the meeting should decide whether to plan it alone or whether a small committee would do a better job. In some cases, the task leader will plan the meeting and determine the objectives on his own. At other times, he will want to involve others so that there is more input into the agenda. It can be helpful to have several people involved.

Here is an example of a preliminary agenda that you might draft and then circulate to your planning group ahead of time:

> The purpose of this meeting is to plan the orientation session for the students and clients. At the end of the meeting we should know the following:
>
> - What kind of introduction is needed and who will do it
> - Which icebreaker activities to do
> - Which refreshments to provide
> - Who is responsible for each activity and its refreshments
> - Who is responsible for informing everyone of where to meet and what to expect

Arrange a time for the key people to meet and develop the agenda. In some cases, the planning of the meeting may need to be done through e-mail, but face-to-face meetings are always best if they can be arranged. When you meet, do the following:

- Ask for input about the purpose and objectives of the meeting from the people who will be involved. Make certain that the objectives describe the outcomes that are expected from the meeting.
- Assign roles for the meeting. Who will be the task leader? Who will be the social leader? The meeting manager? The minute taker?
- Determine who should be at the meeting. Invite only the people who *must* be there so that you don't waste anyone else's time.
- Organize a schedule of events for the meeting.
- Start the meeting with a task that all the participants will take part in. This will ensure that when the participants are on time, there will be something for them to do right away.
- Next to each major topic, write in what type of action is needed or what the expected output is (such as a decision, a vote, an assignment of a task). Write a time estimate next to each topic.
- Do not overload the agenda, and be willing to modify it if items take longer to resolve than expected. Schedule the most critical items first in case your time estimates are not accurate and in case other items need to be saved for another time.
- Post the agenda or distribute it as a handout so that the participants can see it at all times. The sample agenda in figure 2.2 can be used as a model for your own. All items will be conducted by the task leader unless otherwise noted.

A good agenda is the foundation for an efficient and effective meeting.

February 26, 3:00 – 4:15 p.m., Room 123, Brown Building

Task leader: Sarah

Social leader: Joe

Meeting manager: Shanya

Minutes: Mike

3:00 Call to order and welcome.

3:05 Review and approve minutes from the previous meeting.

3:10 Review the agenda and make any necessary changes.

3:12 Brain puzzle activity (Joe).

3:20 Report from ad hoc committee for project mission and goals (Janeen).

- Approve mission and goals, or decide on next steps if the group is not ready to vote.

3:35 Discuss details for next Friday's agency visit (Damon).

- Identify what still needs to be done and who will do it.

3:45 Reports on action items from last meeting:

- Marketing (Dave)
- Equipment (Brittany)
- Fundraising (Brent)

4:00 Identify agenda items for the next meeting.

4:05 Evaluate meeting.

4:15 Adjourn.

Figure 2.2 Sample meeting agenda.

Opening the Meeting

The people running the meeting should arrive ahead of time. Early is on time, on time is late, and late is unacceptable. If you want people to respect the process, be organized and ready when the meeting is supposed to begin. Keep the following points in mind:

- Always start on time. This shows respect for those who arrived on time, and it subtly reminds latecomers that the start time was meant to be taken seriously.
- The social leader should welcome everyone and make sure they know that refreshments are available.
- The task leader should review the agenda and then allow the participants to ask questions and to modify the agenda if necessary.
- The task leader should acknowledge the students who are serving as social leader, minute taker, and meeting manager.
- The meeting manager should remind the participants that the class has set ground rules, which are posted (see page 30 for more information on setting ground rules). She should also remind everyone of the four guidelines for a successful meeting: participate, maintain focus, maintain momentum, and reach closure.

The people running the meeting (the meeting manager, task leader, and social leader) must take their responsibilities seriously; it will set the tone for everything that follows. It is a good idea to rotate people through these roles so that everyone has a chance to fulfill a leadership role.

Facilitating Discussion

The task leader is essentially a facilitator. Her job is to set the tone and to move the agenda forward. Participants don't want to be driven; they want to be led. A good leader keeps the meeting on track by being firm, fair, and consistent. Listen well, think clearly, and speak calmly.

Enthusiasm and good humor are the best tools for setting a positive tone. The task leader can convey enthusiasm through her voice, gestures, and body language. A tone of relaxed humor can be set by starting the meeting with an appropriate story or joke. A humorous icebreaker can do the same when time allows.

Managing the time is another important job of the task leader. This can be difficult—time always seems to run out before tasks are finished. Since the task leader is focused on the task at hand, the meeting manager should assist the task leader by watching the clock. The meeting manager should tell everyone when the meeting is getting off track in terms of time or topic. If the group is off schedule, inform them and ask for their input as to a resolution. Examples of resolutions are postponing the discussion of various items until another meeting, ending discussion and calling a vote, setting up a smaller ad hoc committee to gather information or to resolve a problem, or asking the teacher to make a decision for the group.

The meeting manager encourages the class to follow the ground rules by calling attention to disrespectful comments and poor listening.

The minute taker's job is to make note of all the decisions that are made during the meeting. It is especially important to note who has agreed to do what and by when they will do it.

Meetings often slow down when participants discuss the details of relatively unimportant items. By using the discussion guidelines included here, the task leader can keep the group focused and move the meeting along. Rely on your agenda—that is the reason you made it up ahead of time. Sometimes an agenda needs to be revisited during a meeting. When it does, the task leader may ask the group to decide whether it wants to modify the agenda. It's best to let the group decide because a modified agenda often means that more meetings will need to be scheduled.

Documentation and Follow-Up

One of the biggest problems with meetings is that there is often a lot of talk but little action. Leave 5 to 10 minutes at the end of the meeting for evaluation. It will help you make sure that important items are followed up. During this time, the meeting manager should ask each student to rank the meeting from 1 to 5, with 5 as the highest. Allow each member to briefly explain his response. When the students are finished, the teacher should rate the meeting and give his or her input.

The minute taker should review all actions, assignments, and deadlines. It is even better if the minute taker asks students to restate the assignments, actions, and deadlines they have agreed to. This helps maintain momentum. The minute taker should also indicate which items should be on the next agenda, and she can tell

© BananaStock

Relying on the agenda and practicing proven discussion guidelines can help keep meetings on track.

everyone when and where the meeting minutes will be available.

The task leader should ask for input as to the purpose, time, and tasks for the next meeting. She should end the meeting on time, and she should end it on a positive note by expressing confidence in the group's progress and motivation.

Now your meeting is over. Everyone knows what has been decided, and they know who is supposed to do what and by when they should do it!

Brainstorming

Brainstorming is a technique your team can use both for generating ideas and for solving problems. Brainstorming puts the notion of "two minds are better than one" into action. The first idea that comes to a person's mind isn't always the best one. The brainstorming process allows a team to benefit from thinking as a group.

Here's a guide to the brainstorming process:

1. Select a person to lead the discussion and another to serve as a recorder (the same person *can* do both jobs, but it's a good idea to use two people).
2. Describe the problem to be solved. Make sure that everyone understands the issue.
3. Set a time limit for the brainstorming session.
4. Determine how the best idea will be chosen. Will it be up to the teacher? Should it be voted on? Does the entire group need to agree on a solution? It's quickest to have one person decide, but when you need the group to feel good about a solution, a vote or consensus is better.
5. The recorder should give a copy of the following ground rules to everyone before the meeting begins:
   - Everyone should contribute.
   - Do not evaluate or judge anyone's idea.
   - There are no right or wrong answers.
   - Think outside the box—wild ideas are okay.
   - It's good to build on another person's ideas.
6. The leader makes sure that everyone contributes. He or she also stops participants from criticizing someone else's ideas or from evaluating ideas prematurely.
7. The recorder writes down every idea unless one is repeated.
8. At the end of the session, group similar ideas together. Evaluate what you have; eliminate ideas that clearly won't work and determine which ideas are worth pursuing. See the section titled Problem Solving and Decision Making for more ideas on making these decisions.

After the brainstorming session, you will want to make sure that action is taken on the good ideas. Make sure there is a clear, written record of what was discussed and decided on (see item 8). Then determine who will use the results of the brainstorming to create a specific task with an expected outcome and deadline. Since smaller groups can work more efficiently, the job is often given to a small, temporary committee called an *ad hoc committee* whose assignment is to take action and report to the larger group. In some cases, the ad hoc committee will consist of just one or two individuals; at other times it will be larger depending on the amount of work and on the number of diverse views. In the latter case, the ad hoc committee should have at least one person representing each diverse view.

Have the ad hoc committee report back to the larger group at a predetermined time. For example, your class may use the brainstorming process to generate ideas for a mission and values statement. The ad hoc committee would take the group's ideas, draft a mission and values statement, and then present the statement to the class for further discussion and approval. This process is efficient because not everyone in the class has to help write the draft, but everyone has the opportunity to contribute ideas at the beginning and end of the process.

Problem Solving and Decision Making

Solving problems and making decisions are two important group-process skills to learn. Problems *will* arise in the course of your service-learning project. Most problems are simple, such as "What will we have for lunch?" Some, however, are more complex and require creative solutions. The process outlined in this section is for complicated problems. It's good to gather a few key people together to resolve these problems; two minds are better than one.

1. **Describe the problem in detail.** Some problems are vague. It's a mistake to devise a solution before you gather the relevant information. For example, you find out that the school van will not be available to take the class to the service-learning site tomorrow. An important event will take place at the site tomorrow, so you need alternative transportation. Gather the relevant information: Who has information about the school's transportation guidelines? Who in authority would be willing to help? How many people need to be transported and at what times? If we can't get transportation, what else can we do?

2. **Solve one part of the problem at a time.** Write out a list of what you need to know first, second, third, and so on. When the problem is time sensitive—that is, when there is a deadline—determine when decisions must be made and acted on. In the previous example, you first need to explore alternative transportation. You also need to establish a cutoff time for when you will have to reschedule the event if you have not found transportation. If you haven't, how will the rescheduling be handled?

3. **Check your assumptions.** As you look for a solution, use each other to check and recheck your assumptions. In the haste to find a solution, people sometimes become blind to the obvious, and they move forward without good information. In the previous example, the bus driver said that the bus was not available and that there was no other bus. Is there someone else at the school who might have more information?

4. **Brainstorm.** Brainstorm with your group to generate creative solutions. Sometimes thinking outside the box will generate some new options that were not obvious before.

5. **Make a list of possible solutions.** List the possible solutions and write down the advantages and disadvantages of each.

6. **Make a decision.** There are several ways to make a decision. You can ask an authority, such as your teacher, to decide. You can have the class vote. You can also talk about the options and tweak your solutions until everyone agrees on a solution. One way to make a quick decision *and* to have everyone feel ownership is to have one person, such as the teacher or a trusted classmate, make the final decision with input from the group.

Establishing Ground Rules

Many group projects are characterized by an imbalance of effort; certain students do a lot more work than others. You can prevent this to some degree by having the students and the teacher work seriously on setting and agreeing to clearly articulated ground rules.

Every team needs to set its own ground rules because rules are specific to each situation and group of people. It is important for the entire team to participate in creating the ground rules so that everyone feels a sense of ownership and has a clear understanding of the guidelines. (An important aspect of setting ground rules is understanding how a professional behaves. The sidebar Showing Professionalism on page 32 provides students with a behavior-specific list of how professionals conduct themselves. You may want to have this list available as you determine your ground rules.)

AP Images/Alden Pellett

It takes cooperation to solve complex problems.

One way to set ground rules is by answering the following questions (Petzoldt 1974):

1. How should individuals treat each other one on one?
2. What responsibilities does each person have to the group?
3. What responsibilities does the group have to the individuals?

To answer the three questions, the entire class should brainstorm ideas. Make sure that the ideas get recorded on a white board, chalkboard, or flip chart that everyone can see. Your teacher usually facilitates this discussion. As you work through the questions, urge everyone to elaborate on each idea by using behaviorally descriptive phrases. This is extremely important; if your ground rules contain phrases that are too general, students won't understand how they are expected to behave. For example, when answering the question "How should individuals treat each other?" a common response is "We should treat each other with respect." Of course, respect is important, but you must go into greater depth. Do this by answering specific questions such as "What specific actions show respect for your classmates?" Responses might include the following: "Listening when others are speaking," "Addressing problems and conflicts right away," "Not talking about people behind their backs."

1. Individual to individual. Here is your chance to set the ground rules for how individuals should treat each other. Examples of topics include respect, and specific actions that show respect; active listening, such as using eye contact and restating messages; and using assertive communication and "I" statements to address problems promptly.

2. Individual to group. Clarify the responsibilities that each individual has to the group. These important rules allow the teacher and students to hold each other accountable. Examples of areas that are typically discussed are showing up for class prepared and on time, finishing work on time, telling the class ahead of time if someone cannot finish his work on time, giving a best effort in all work, asking for help, and giving good compliments.

3. Group to individual. Describe the responsibilities that the class as a whole has to each student. Topics that are typically discussed are pitching in to help others without complaint, trying to let everyone work on the tasks they like the most, making sure everyone has meaningful work to do, letting people do their work in their own creative way, making sure everyone knows the ground rules, and making sure that information and opportunities are available to everyone so that the assignment of tasks is fair and equal.

It is useless to spend time setting ground rules if those rules are not followed. The following strategies for making your ground rules work for you are suggested by EdChange in Guide for Setting Ground Rules (n.d.):

1. Post the ground rules where where they will be visible during the entire course.
2. Challenge each other on ground rules early and often. Ask your teacher to challenge you on the ground rules too. If you do not set a tone of strict adherence to the rules early on, it may be impossible to enforce them later.
3. If you know that one or more ground rules is about to apply to a particular situation, bring it to the group's attention just prior

to that situation. For example, if you are about to conduct a meeting, you may want to remind everyone about the group's commitment to active listening and to "I" statements.

4. If the class is regularly breaking a ground rule, raise the issue in class and discuss what should be done.
5. Revisit your ground rules occasionally. If time allows, ask the class whether anyone would like to make changes.
6. Setting ground rules can also be an essential activity for students to do with clients in the initial stage of a service-learning project. This is especially true when the clients are from a background that differs from the students' (see appendix B for activities).

Showing Professionalism

Learning how to act professionally is just as important to being a good student as it is to being a good future employee. Professionalism is learned, and standards for professional behavior provide a basis for self-evaluation and feedback. The self-evaluation form in table 2.3 describes specific professional behaviors. You can use this form to evaluate your own professionalism. It can also help the group decide on ground rules, and it can can serve as criteria for constructive feedback. The evaluation form can be used as it is or it can be modified.

Table 2.3 Self-Evaluation of Professionalism

Instructions: Rate yourself in each of the following areas. Using a five-point rating scale, grade yourself on your overall professionalism. Nobody is perfect, but this chart can help you understand exactly how you should act as you participate in the service-learning project.

Scoring:

5 = I do this very consistently

4 = I do this most of the time, but I could do a little better

3 = I sometimes do these things and sometimes I don't

2 = I rarely do these things

1 = I never do these things

There are 10 categories. Take each rating, multiply by 2, and then add up the ratings to get your total score out of 100 percent. The score will categorize your rating of professionalism as that of either an A, B, C, D, or F student.

I show a high level of commitment to the service-learning project by • attending class and meetings on time, • coming to class or to the project site prepared, with ideas and resources, • contributing to class discussions, and • volunteering to accept responsibility.	Rating: ____ × 2 = ______ Score Comments:
I show a high level of teamwork by • working closely with others to complete tasks and meet objectives, • keeping the commitments I make, and • following the ground rules set by our class.	Rating: ____ × 2 = ______ Score Comments:
I demonstrate excellent leadership skills by • helping run class meetings, • getting other people involved, • presenting a positive outlook, and • setting an example that others can follow.	Rating: ____ × 2 = ______ Score Comments:

I show a high commitment to learning the necessary information and skills by • reading this book, • asking good questions, • seeking out resources and information, • seeking constructive criticism, and • offering ideas for improvement.	Rating: ____ × 2 = ______ Score Comments:
I demonstrate good problem-solving and decision-making skills by • taking the initiative to identify problems, • seeking assistance to make sure that problems are resolved, and • showing good judgment when dealing with problems.	Rating: ____ × 2 = ______ Score Comments:
I appear professional at all times by • dressing for the occasion; • using good communication skills with classmates, clients, and teacher; and • accepting constructive criticism and making necessary changes.	Rating: ____ × 2 = ______ Score Comments:
I use the class's resources wisely by • using money only for approved purchases, • taking good care of equipment, • not wasting supplies, and • thinking of creative ways to save time and money.	Rating: ____ × 2 = ______ Score Comments:
I demonstrate excellent oral and written communication skills by • using "I" statements, • listening well, • speaking up when necessary and asking for clarification, and • using proper grammar and spelling.	Rating: ____ × 2 = ______ Score Comments:
I complete all assigned tasks • on time, • with the utmost attention to quality and detail, and • I have someone else check my work in order to make sure that it has been done correctly.	Rating: ____ × 2 = ______ Score Comments:
I consider myself important to the overall success of our service-learning project because I • have made major contributions, • always have a can-do attitude, • pay attention to the needs and wants of others (i.e., of clients and classmates), and • am considered by others to be dependable.	Rating: ____ × 2 = ______ Score Comments:
	Total score: ______/100 A = 90 D = 60 B = 80 F = 59 or lower C = 70

TEAM DEVELOPMENT AND LEADERSHIP STYLES

When students or employees work on group projects, they tend to use their time inefficiently because have not been taught how to work in groups (Blanchard and Carew 1996). Learning the stages of team development and their corresponding leadership styles will help your team function better.

A group is a collection of individuals who share a common interest—a class of students, for example. But in order for a group of students to be considered a team, those students must learn how to work together. In a group, the efforts of individuals are cumulative: 1 + 1 = 2. In a team, with people working together, the efforts of individuals are amplified and 1 + 1 becomes greater than 2. On the flip side, conflict in a group can detract from everyone's efforts. In this case, 1 + 1 is less than 2.

The stages of team development and their corresponding leadership styles are illustrated and explained in table 2.4. This table gives an ideal scenario of how your classmates and teacher might interact throughout the service-learning project. We'll discuss how you can interpret these stages of team development and their corresponding leadership styles as well as how team development and leadership can work together.

Understanding the Stages of Team Development

Your class will start off as a group of individuals who are unfamiliar with each other, but they can become a close-knit team. Along the way, there are five stages of development that can be

Table 2.4 Team Development and Leadership Model

Stages of team development	Suggested activities for each step of the service project	Corresponding leadership styles
Beginning At the start of your class, you will not know each other or what to expect. You will be open to information, but you will not know what to do yet.	**Step 1** • List the learning goals and objectives. • Agency site visit and contracting • Break the ice and have diversity-awareness activities. **Step 2** • Begin learning about team building. **Step 3** • Begin planning the specifics of your service project.	**Guide** The teacher will facilitate the beginning of your service project. She will help you get comfortable with your project, help you become a high-performing team, and give you the information you need to plan your project.
Sorting As your class starts the project, expect some confusion or conflicts. This is to be expected as students learn about what to do and how to do it. In this stage it might feel like you are not getting anywhere, but continue working on Steps 1, 2, and 3. You will begin to feel comfortable with the project.	**Step 2** • Establish ground rules. • Learn about team development. • Learn to conduct effective and efficient meetings. • Complete the Showing Professionalism evaluation. • Facilitate good communication and conflict resolution. **Step 3** • Write a mission statement. • Complete the task sheets. • Create a project timeline.	**Catalyst** The teacher will be sort of like a cheerleader. He will encourage you to move forward, help the class resolve problems and conflicts, and make sure you have the information and resources you need.

Stages of team development	Suggested activities for each step of the service project	Corresponding leadership styles
Achieving Once you and your classmates have developed a commitment to the project, good relationships with each other and with the clients, and an understanding of your goals and roles, you will start taking the initiative and you will start doing things for yourselves.	**Step 4** • Conduct efficient and effective meetings. • Conduct your service project. • Continue following ground rules and using good communication skills. Review standards for professionalism. • Follow through on task worksheets; stick to the timeline. • Ask for assistance in terms of resources, feedback, and other support.	**Partner** The teacher will now serve as a partner who is helping you by providing the resources, feedback, and support you need to do your project. She will not do things for you that you can and should do for yourself.
Excelling Not all teams get to this point, but some do. This is where a team is doing extremely well, as is evident from the group's creativity, relaxed attitudes, and high productivity.	**Step 4** • Continue all tasks of the achieving team, but allow students to take the initiative as much as possible. • Continue to pay attention to ground rules, good communication, and professionalism. • Value each person's creative contributions to the team effort.	**Supporter** If your class gets to this stage, your teacher will take more of a back seat and will let you do most everything on your own. Even when you are making a mistake, she will let you learn from it, provided you have the skills to do so.
Ending As you near the end of the service project, you will be ready for closure, reflection, and evaluation. Your teacher will help you select specific assignments that will facilitate the reflection process.	**Step 5** • Celebrate with those you have helped during your project. Acknowledge how they have helped you. • Complete the evaluations. • Complete the reflection activities.	**Guide** At this stage your teacher will resume the role of a guide and she will provide specific activities to complete. She will make sure that the appropriate closure, reflection, and evaluation take place.

Adapted from Blanchard and Carew 1996; Blanchard and Hersey 1996; Tuckman and Jensen 1977.

anticipated, recognized, and addressed. During stage 1, the beginning, the group is a collection of individuals who are getting to know each other. During stage 2, sorting, it is natural for your group to experience conflict. This conflict can be good because it means that people care, that they are working through important issues, and that they are becoming a team. When you reach stages 3 and 4, achieving and excelling, your team is functioning and working well. The final stage, the ending, stage 5, is when the team reflects on and reviews what members have learned and when it prepares to disband.

Understanding Corresponding Leadership Styles

There isn't a best leadership style because the appropriate style depends on which stage of team development the class is in. The leadership style of guide, in which the teacher or student-leader serves as a task-oriented facilitator, works best with a team that is at the beginning or ending of the cycle. The leadership style of catalyst, in which the teacher or student-leader takes an active coaching role, will help the class move through stage 2, sorting. The leadership styles of partnering and supporting work well with stages 3 and 4, achieving and excelling.

How Team Development and Leadership Styles Work Together

The concept of readiness is critical to how a leader and a team can best work together on a project. Readiness can be defined as the team's motivation and ability to complete a portion of the service-learning project. It is important to understand how motivation and ability work together to determine the class's readiness. A common error with group projects is to interpret a student's uncertainty and apprehension as a lack of motivation. A person's willingness to work will change as his confidence, commitment, and motivation change. Therefore, the key to a successful group project is to build your confidence, commitment, and motivation by working through the five stages of team development.

Keep in mind that each student comes to class with her own motivations and skills. Everyone can grow in knowledge and ability through the project. One student who appears unwilling to work may in fact be very committed and motivated to do the project, but he might be insecure about what to do or about his ability to do the work. Another student may know a great deal and may have plenty of ability, but she may not feel motivated or committed. Early involvement with the clients in step 1, working with the class team in step 2, and seeing the big picture during step 3 should help build a commitment to the team and to the service-learning project.

Management Resources

The Free Management Library provides comprehensive resources on leadership and management. Over the past 10 years, the Library has grown into one of the world's largest and best-organized collections of these resources. Go to www.managementhelp.org/index.html to view the large list of topics and resources that are available to your team.

SUMMARY

Learning to work as a team is essential. Students can learn how to work as a team through the process of completing the service-learning project. The project can turn into a nightmare, however, if a good team is not in place.

Since we can safely assume that students in the health, physical education, and recreation professions are motivated to help others, it is likely that the majority of them will be effective, motivated team members. If a few classmates won't engage no matter what you try, remember that people get out of a project what they put into it. Don't let someone else sidetrack your learning experience.

REFERENCES

Blanchard, K.H., and D. Carew. 1996. How to get your group to perform like a team. *Training and Development* 50 (9):34–37.

Blanchard, K.H., and P. Hersey. 1996. Great ideas revisited. *Training and Development* 50 (1):42–47.

Ed Change n.d. Guide for setting ground rules. Retrieved from the Multicultural Pavilion from Paul C. Gorski and EdChange Web site: www.edchange.org/multicultural/activities/groundrules.html

Free Management Library. 1997-2008. Managing meetings. www.managementhelp.org/grp_skll/meetings/meetings.htm.

Hathaway, P. 1990. Giving and receiving criticism: Your key to interpersonal success. *The Change Agent* Menlo Park, CA: Crisp.

La Guardia, J.G., and R.M. Ryan. 2002. What adolescents need: A self-determination theory perspective on development within families, school, and society. In F. Pajares and T. Urdan (Eds.), *Academic motivation of adolescents*, 193–219. Greenwich, CT: Information Age.

McNamara, C. n.d. Habits to differentiate good from poor listening. www.managementhelp.org/commskls/listen/gd_vs_pr.htm.

Mitchell, A.V., and J.F. Meier. 1983. *Camp counseling: Leadership and programming for the organized camp* (6th ed.). Philadelphia: Saunders.

PAR Group. 2007. The secrets to listening well. www.thepargroup.com/article_SecretsListenWell.html.

Petzoldt, P. 1974. *The wilderness handbook*. New York: Norton.

Ready, R., and K. Burton. 2004. *Neuro-linguistic programming for dummies*. Chichester, West Sussex, England: Wiley.

Tuckman, B.W. and M.A. Jensen. 1977. Stages of small group development revisited. *Group & Organizational Studies* 2 (4):419–427.

Wertheim, E.G. n.d. The importance of effective communication. http://web.cba.neu.edu/~ewertheim/interper/commun.htm.

REFLECTION

In addition to writing in a journal, a useful activity for reflection is What My Team Looks Like. This activity takes about 50 minutes. You'll need large pieces of paper or poster board (about half of a poster board is enough), a collection of old magazines, glue sticks, markers, and scissors. Ask everyone to think about the members of the team. What strengths, diverse talents, and special qualities do they bring to the group? Then consider what it might look like if this group of individuals were to become a high-functioning team serving the community. The students should leaf through the magazines in order to find images that remind them of their vision for the team. They should then cut out and arrange those pictures on the poster board. Use the markers to add color and any words that come to mind. When the posters are finished, have each person talk about his or her poster. This activity can get your team off to a great start by creating a positive vision of what you will accomplish together.

STUDENT CHECKLIST

Use this checklist anytime your class has a communication or group-process need. It will help you determine which activity or information section you should refer to.

- ☐ If people are not communicating well, do the "Practicing Communication Skills" activity.
- ☐ If there is too much drama or if cliques are forming, do the "Establishing Ground Rule"s activity.
- ☐ If meetings seem to be a waste of time or if issues are not being resolved, review and implement the guidelines for conducting effective and efficient meetings.
- ☐ If complicated problems arise, try applying problem-solving and decision-making strategies and brainstorming.
- ☐ If students are behaving unprofessionally, complete the "How to Show Professionalism" self-evaluation.
- ☐ If some students appear unmotivated, use active listening to find out if they are uncertain about what to do or if they are uninterested in the project or both. If you can figure out what is missing (e.g., direction, skills, commitment), try to fix it by reviewing and applying the suggestions in the Team Development and Leadership section.

STEP

3

Planning the Project

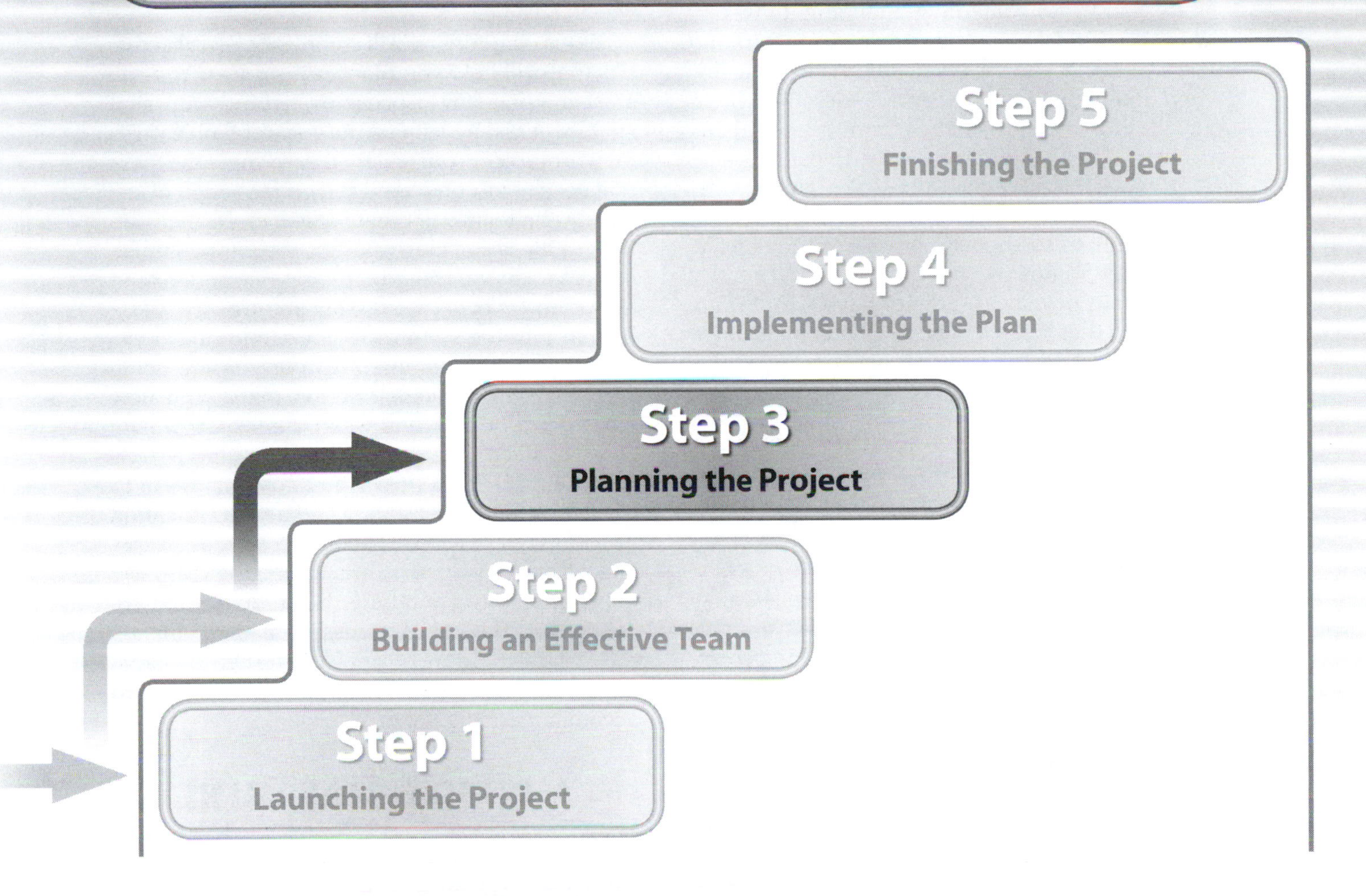

In this step you will

- **write your project's mission statement,**
- **prepare goals and objectives,**
- **determine timelines and tasks, and**
- **define team members' roles.**

> **You can't overestimate the need to plan and prepare. In most of the mistakes I've made, there has been this common theme of inadequate planning beforehand. You really can't over-prepare in business!**
>
> *—Chris Corrigan*

It's much more fun to do something than it is to plan to do something. Planning, however, is essential for any group project. Without it, no one will know who needs to do what by when. Planning helps students understand their contributions to a project and thereby helps them manage their time appropriately. Because we're all busy, we put off doing work if we don't see the urgency in doing it right now. Planning is a way for students to see how their actions today pave the road for tomorrow.

The main problem students have with group projects is that just a few people usually do most of the work. This typically occurs for one of two reasons:

1. Students are scared—inactive because they don't know what they are supposed to do, how they are supposed to do it, or when it needs to be done.
2. Students may not be committed to or really care about the class or the service-learning project. As a result, critical tasks are not finished on time, conflicts arise, and people feel stress.

That's why planning is critical for your project's success. Planning reduces stress, improves learning, and produces a better project. When you plan ahead, you know what to do each day, and you realize that what you do today determines whether you succeed tomorrow. The planning process helps you see both the big picture of the project and everyone's role in making it a success. It also helps you feel more committed to the project.

Planning helps you manage your time by making you think about how far ahead you should start each task. For example, if you are conducting a workshop, you may need to advertise for the event, register participants, recruit volunteers, solicit donations, and so on. These tasks don't get done overnight. You will need to start work well in advance.

In this chapter you will complete several activities that will help you plan your project. You will start the planning process by writing a mission statement and by refining the goals and objectives for your project. You will then determine the tasks that need to be completed and create action plans. Finally, the team will create a flow chart that lists the deadlines and illustrates the steps for completing tasks. The chart will help everyone understand how their tasks fit into the big picture.

Your mission statement, goals, and objectives will provide the details of where you are going and why. The checklist, action plans, and flow chart describe how and when the project will be completed. For example, if your class has agreed to write a grant for the county school system to fund after-school recreation and health education programs, you will need to conduct a needs assessment. The students who are writing the grant will not be able to write it until the students who are conducting the needs assessment have finished their task. If there are delays with the needs assessment, the team will need to adjust the timeline to accommodate the delay.

MISSION STATEMENT

Your class needs a clear and concise mission statement for your service-learning project. The statement should describe the project, what it hopes to accomplish, and what your values are. Ideally, the students, the teacher, and several client representatives should help write the statement. A good mission statement will inspire commitment, innovation, and courage. This is not easy to do, but it is worthwhile because people will work extra hard for something they believe in. Use the following activity to guide your team in writing a mission statement.

Write Your Mission Statement

You start writing your mission statement by brainstorming general ideas. Then, you prepare a rough draft. You complete your mission statement by refining the draft into the precise language that conveys the intent of your project.

➤ *Clarify and Brainstorm*

When your class meets to draft a mission statement, begin the meeting by clarifying what you want your mission statement to do. Your mission statement should have the following criteria:

- Express the project's purpose in a way that inspires support and commitment.
- Motivate the students, teacher, and clients.
- Be convincing and easy to grasp.
- Use active verbs to describe what you do.
- Avoid jargon.
- Be clear and concise so that anyone not connected to the service-learning project could easily understand what the project is about.

Start the process of drafting a mission statement by answering the following three questions. Ask students, teachers, and clients to list any words, phrases, or ideas that come to mind. Do not edit at this point. Give everyone a chance to be heard. Look for language and concepts that everyone seems to agree with.

1. What are the needs that we need to address? (That is, what is the purpose of the service-learning project?)

   ____

   ____

   ____

   ____

   ____

2. What should we do to address these needs? (That is, what is the product or program your class will provide?)

   ____

   ____

   ____

   ____

   ____

3. What principles or beliefs guide our work? (That is, what are the values you associate with your project?)

   ____

   ____

   ____

   ____

   ____

➤ *Draft Your Mission Statement*

As a group, review the following sample mission statement. It answers the three questions you just asked.

> The purpose of the recreation conference is to facilitate networking and the exchange of current, relevant information and resources for students and professionals in the recreation and leisure professions. Toward this end, we provide
>
> - programs in a variety of areas, including recreational therapy, commercial recreation and tourism, outdoor recreation, and community recreation;
> - a mix of informational sessions and hands-on workshops; and
> - networking opportunities between students, teachers, and practitioners.
>
> We value
>
> - meeting the needs of both students and professionals;
> - providing all interested persons access to our program through advertising, easy registration, and accurate, convenient travel information;
> - adhering to a standard of excellence in everything we do; and
> - working as a high-functioning team, having fun, and learning while we conduct our project.

As a class, review the results of your brainstorming process, and draft a mission statement by choosing the ideas that are important to you. Consider the categories of purpose, product, and values.

➤ *Refine Your Mission Statement*

Select several students to serve on an ad hoc committee that will refine the results into a mission statement. The committee will present the statement to the class for its input and approval. This ad hoc committee will put the group's ideas into clear and concise language. They will not insert new ideas, but rather make sure that the group's ideas are clearly stated. When the ad hoc committee has revised the mission statement, they should again present the statement to the class for its input and approval.

Copy the final mission statement here so that you can refer to it easily.

____

____

____

____

____

____

____

____

➤ *Keep Your Mission Statement Visible*

The mission statement should be posted in a prominent place. It will serve as a reminder of what your class is working on and why. If it's well written, it will guide the students as they make decisions about the project. Where you post your mission statement will depend on your school. If possible, post it in your classroom. If not, there may be a bulletin board where you can display the mission and other information about your project. If there is no place to post the mission statement, consider having each student keep a copy of it in the front of his or her class notebook. A Web site for your project would be a great place to display it too, if that's okay with your school.

GOALS AND OBJECTIVES

In 1974, David Campbell wrote a self-help book titled *If You Don't Know Where You're Going, You'll Probably End Up Somewhere Else*. This sentiment is still true. Goals and objectives point a group in the direction it wishes to go. Without them, the students would all go in different directions. Goals and objectives also serve as the basis for evaluating your project.

The mission statement, goals, and objectives are different yet related. Generally speaking, a mission statement is the broadest, most general description of your project. Goals are a product of the mission statement, and they provide details about what the group hopes to accomplish. Objectives follow from the goals, and they are detailed, specific, and often measurable. Typically there are several goals for the project, and each goal has several objectives that describe specifically what must be done to accomplish that goal.

Consider this example of the purpose portion of a hypothetical mission statement:

> The purpose of our service-learning project is to improve the health of low-income residents of southeastern Ohio.

The goals that elaborate on this mission statement should describe, in general terms, what steps should be taken to accomplish the mission. Each goal should be a general statement describing what needs to happen to make the mission a reality. Here are six sample goals for the mission statement.

1. Identify the health needs of low-income individuals who are receiving services from the Athens County Health Department.
2. Identify the available resources in the region that could meet these needs.
3. Create literature that would educate residents about existing programs that can meet both their immediate and long-term health needs.
4. Design at least one new health education program that would meet an identified need that is not being met by existing services.
5. Implement the new health education programs at one or more locations in Athens County.
6. Evaluate the new health education program and literature, and then make recommendations for future health services and health education efforts in the Athens County area.

While reading these goals, you may have noticed that each one begins with a descriptive verb. Well-written goals and objectives contain verbs that specifically describe the action you hope to accomplish. Bloom's taxonomy for educational objectives contains many verbs in three main categories, which are called *domains*. Goals and objectives in the cognitive domain involve knowledge and the development of intellectual (thinking) skills. Goals and objectives in the psychomotor domain involve physical movement, coordination, and motor (doing) skills. Goals and objectives in the affective domain involve emotional-coping skills (feelings, values, and attitudes). Applying Bloom's taxonomy to the writing of goals and objectives does not have to be difficult. Table 3.1 provides examples of terms, from simple to complex, from the taxonomy, which will be useful for writing your service-learning objectives (Clark 2007). Keep this list handy while you write the objectives. Also refer to Donald Clark's Web site at www.nwlink.com/~donclark/hrd/bloom.html for more examples in all three domains.

Now it is time to look at the final, most specific step: objectives. Good objectives are challenging to write because in order to be useful, they must contain three elements (Mager 1997):

1. Performance—a statement that describes what the students are expected to do or produce
2. Conditions—a statement that describes the important conditions (if any) that must be present if the performance is to occur
3. Criteria—wherever possible, an objective describes the criteria for an acceptable performance by describing how well the task must be done

Bob Mager (1997) shares the following tips. If you would like to see more detailed instructions and practice exercises, refer to his book.

- Use words that are open to little interpretation. For example, instead of using terms such as *to understand* and *to appreciate*, use descriptive words such as *to identify* or *to compare*. Bloom's taxonomy provides specific examples of verbs to use.

Table 3.1 Bloom's Taxonomy for Service-Learning Goals and Objectives

Category	Descriptive verbs in order of simple to complex
Cognitive (thinking) skills	• define, describe • explain, summarize • apply, produce • analyze, illustrate, compare, contrast • integrate, compile
Affective (feelings, values, attitudes) skills	• asks, names • participates, helps • proposes, justifies • integrates, defends • displays, revises
Psychomotor (physical) skills	• sort, select • volunteers, explains • assembles, organizes • adapts, reorganizes • designs, builds, creates

Reprinted, by permission, from D. Clark. Available: http://www.nwlink.com/~donclark/hrd/bloom.html.

- When writing about the performance, consider what you will be doing or producing as you accomplish this objective.
- To write about the conditions, think about what resources you will need in order to accomplish the performance and produce the product.
- To write about criteria, describe an acceptable product or performance.

Here are some sample objectives for the first goal. Can you identify the performance, conditions, and criteria in each of these objectives?

Goal 1: Identify the health needs of low-income residents who are receiving services from the Athens County Health Department.

Sample Objectives

1. Design a health needs survey that is consistent with the standards of other community health needs surveys and with appendix A. The survey should gather information about the immediate and long-term health needs of low-income Athens County residents.
2. Administer the health needs survey to a random sample of low-income Athens County residents who are currently receiving services from the Athens County Health Department.
3. Analyze the survey data using SPSS software.
4. Based on the survey results, write a report about the immediate and long-term health needs of low-income Athens County residents.

The following activity will guide you in writing goals and objectives.

Write Your Goals and Objectives

Goals and objectives should be prepared with input from the teacher, the students, and one or more client representatives. In the interest of time, your team may want to appoint a subcommittee to prepare a draft of goals and objectives, which can then be brought to the class for its input and modification.

➤ *Write Goals*

You should already have a good idea about what the project's goals are from the work the class has already completed. Before you start writing your final goals, review the following:

- Learning goals and objectives (completed during step 1, page 5)
- The final commitment you have made with the agency (completed during step 1, page 12)
- Your mission statement

Write your goals in the space provided on pages 45 to 47. Double-check your goals to determine whether any of the action verbs can be improved using Bloom's taxonomy.

➤ *Write Objectives*

Expect to prepare several objectives for each goal, and plan to write several drafts. Start by putting your ideas on paper, and then make each objective more specific. To make each objective more specific, make sure each one contains a description of performance, conditions, and criteria. Here is an example of a first draft of an objective:

> Write a report about the health status of low-income residents in Athens County.

The final objective might look like this:

> Create an accurate, up-to-date, and comprehensive report (as judged by the teacher) on the health status of low-income residents of Athens County. The report should be based on statistics and information that are less than 10 years old and that can be obtained through state and national data banks.

In this case, the performance portion of the objective is "Create a . . . report." The conditions portion is "based on statistics and information that are less than 10 years old and that can be obtained . . . " The criterion portion is "accurate, up-to-date, and comprehensive . . . (as judged by the teacher) . . . "

Goal 1 ____

____

Objectives

a ____

____

____

b ____

____

____

c ____

____

____

d ____

____

____

Goal 2 ____

____

Objectives

a ____

____

____

b ____

____

____

c ____

____

____

d ____

____

____

Goal 3 ____

____

Objectives

a ____

____

____

b ____

____

____

c ____

____

____

d

Goal 4

Objectives

a

b

c

d

Goal 5

Objectives

a

b

c

d

TASKS AND TIMELINES

Any complex project requires organization. The less experience students have, the more organization they need. People who have not planned and implemented complicated projects before may assume that things will just happen or at least that the tasks can be completed at the last minute. Planning major functions, tasks, and timelines is more than a mental exercise; it is vital to know which tasks must be completed before others and to know the deadlines that must be met before the project begins. Consider, for example, a health fair. Your class might want to have posters made that would advertise the event. Those posters would need to be posted a couple of weeks prior to the event. The printer would have deadlines, and volunteers would need to be recruited ahead of time to hang the posters.

Allow plenty of time to organize the project. This will allow everyone to relax as they decide how diverse details will be managed over the course of the project (Russell 1982). The action plans and flow chart you design are like master to-do lists for each student. Overwork leads to problems such as stress and poor work quality. Your plans and chart will help you avoid them. The plans and chart allow for flexibility, but they also keep everyone on task because the students will be able to see that some tasks need to be completed before others and that deadlines will need to be met well before the final project is completed. Here are four tips to assist you in your planning efforts.

1. **If this project has been done before, use information from previous classes as you create your plans.** Often a class will do a service-learning project that is similar to one that was done by a previous class. Review the documents they developed, and adapt them to your project. You might find the checklists, action plans, and flow charts from previous classes particularly useful. Use those documents as guides only. Do not give in to the temptation to adopt the documents exactly as they are.

2. **Keep copies of your planning information in a single notebook or location for easy access** (Russell 1982). You will want to keep all of your planning documents in one place so that the teacher and students can easily locate them. Your ground rules should already be posted in a visible, central location. As you develop your mission statement, goals, action plans, and flow chart, make sure to place them in a central notebook or post them where everyone can easily find them.

3. **Divide complicated tasks into smaller, manageable parts, and rank them according to importance** (Russell 1982). Divide a big job into smaller parts. This makes it easier to plan your time and efforts. For example, if you plan to market your service-learning project, you will have to break the larger task into smaller tasks. Once you have the smaller tasks, you can assign yourself priorities and deadlines for each. When there is a long to-do list, it helps to rank the items according to their importance. Usually the number-one items are the most difficult to start. If you tend to complete the easier items first, the high-priority items may not be completed on time.

4. **Use technology to make the process easier.** Sometimes computer software can make the project easier. You can use word processing and spreadsheet programs to create documents that are professional and easy to edit. Project-planning software packages such as Microsoft Project can help you create flow charts. The use of software is beyond the scope of this text, but depending on your resources and class learning objectives, you may want to explore it further. If your class wants a particular software package, inquire whether the school or teacher can purchase it for your use.

Keep these tips in mind as you create your checklist, action plans, and flow chart. Remember that these documents are critical if everyone is to work together to conduct a successful service-learning project.

Checklist and Action Plans

Create a checklist for the major tasks before you write more specific action plans. This checklist will likely be modified, but it provides a starting point for developing your action plans and flow chart. Once the checklist is completed, you will create action plans for each major task. These action plans provide the details and timeline for the day-to-day tasks so that everyone knows what to do and by when it needs to be done. For example, if the programming committee needs to secure funding and order equipment, they may decide that they need to begin work six weeks before the event.

Checklist

The major tasks for your project will be written down. Typical examples of major tasks include the following:

- Designing programs
- Gathering materials
- Locating and scheduling facilities
- Developing risk-management plans
- Securing transportation
- Recruiting and training volunteers
- Writing and distributing publicity
- Registering clients
- Fundraising
- Developing a budget
- Conducting a needs assessment survey
- Evaluating the program

The exact tasks will depend on your class project. In addition to these major tasks, your class may ask a student project leader to help the teacher facilitate the work of the other students.

An example of a checklist for a college class that is preparing an after-school recreation program is in table 3.2. The checklist your team creates (see activity on page 51) will serve as the basis for creating more detailed action plans and a master flow chart. Note that this checklist is a starting point and that some deadline changes will probably be made when the flow chart is created.

Table 3.2 Sample Checklist for After-School Recreation Programming

Major function	Tasks	Time needed to complete the tasks (in weeks)	Deadline
Competitive sports programming	• Design competitive sports programming lesson plans. • Work with materials and equipment committee. • Train other students to help with programs. • Deliver programs.	8	9/15 ongoing 9/22 10/2-10/27
Noncompetitive sports programming	• Design noncompetitive sports programming lesson plans. • Work with materials and equipment committee. • Train other students to help with programs. • Deliver programs	8	9/15 ongoing 9/22 10/1-10/27
Creative activities programming	• Design creative activities programming lesson plans. • Work with materials and equipment committee. • Train other students to help with programs. • Deliver programs.	8	9/15 ongoing 9/22 10/12-10/27
Scheduling and transportation	• Establish a tentative master calendar. • Meet with classmates and school to confirm dates. • Meet with program and well-being committees to schedule activities. • Confirm facilities and transportation.	4	9/8 9/15 9/20 9/22

(continued)

Table 3.2 ***(continued)***

Major function	Tasks	Time needed to complete the tasks (in weeks)	Deadline
Facilities and risk management	• Survey the available facilities and equipment. • Work with program committees to review risk-management considerations for program activities. • Create a risk-management plan for the facility. • Monitor risk management during events.	8	9/4 9/8 9/15 10/1-10/27
Materials	• Inventory existing equipment and supplies. • Work with programming committees to get materials and supplies by the dates needed.	8	9/8 10/2 and ongoing
Publicity	• Visit with the school's public relations offices. • Visit with local media. • Meet with news reporters.	4	9/12 9/21 10/8
Fundraising and donations	• Meet with programming and well-being committee about needs. • Solicit financial support as well as donations of materials and supplies from local businesses.	6	9/15 9/29 and ongoing
Well-being	• Plan for healthy snacks. • Plan for icebreakers. • Plan for social events. • Plan for meaningful give-away items. • Deliver these during the program. • Plan an end-of-program celebration.	8	9/8 9/8 9/15 9/15 10/2-10/27 10/27
Evaluation	• Create evaluation forms for students, parents, and teachers. • Give out and collect evaluations. • Analyze results. • Create an evaluation report.	4	10/13 10/25 11/3 11/8
Student project leader	• Call class meetings for committee updates. • Keep track of the committee's progress by using action plans and flow charts. • Involve others in troubleshooting, and adjust schedules as needed. • Facilitate communication between the class and the school.	10	ongoing ongoing ongoing ongoing

Create Your Checklist

During a class meeting, use a calendar to create your checklist. Make a list that everyone can see as it is being written. Use, for example, a white board, chalk board, or large piece of paper taped to the wall.

1. Determine the dates for the project to begin and end. Fill in dates, or possible dates, of major events.
2. Brainstorm a list of major tasks. Prioritize the items on the list.
3. Estimate the amount of time that will be needed to finish each task. Determine deadlines using your calendar.

You can use table 3.3 as a checklist for your project, or you can use it as a guide for creating your own checklist form.

Table 3.3 Service-Learning Project Checklist Template

Major function	Tasks	Time needed to complete the tasks (in weeks)	Deadline

After you finish writing the checklist, determine how many people will work in each group and then decide who will work on each item. These smaller groups, or committees, will work on their action plans outside of class. If certain tasks require only a small amount of time, students on those committees may join other committees or take on a new function.

Now you are ready to start the last two planning activities: writing action plans (in committees) and drawing a flow chart (the entire team). The action plans offer a detailed process for executing tasks, and the flow chart is a master timeline for the project.

Action Plans

An action plan is a detailed document that each committee creates to guide its work. Use it to clarify how your committee's goal will be accomplished by deciding who will do what, by when, and what resources they will need. An example of an action plan for the Competitive Sports Programming Committee is in table 3.4. Note that tasks have been broken down into detailed steps so that deadlines can be assigned. Use the activity on page 53 to create your action plan.

Table 3.4 Sample Action Plan for the Competitive Sports Programming Committee

Committee name: Competitive Sports Programming

Members: Jorge, Sun-Li, William, Laura, and Aki

Desired outcome: The goal of the competitive sports programming committee is to choose competitive sports games that are appropriate for the students and that help meet the goals of the school and the service-learning program. The committee will create a programming plan and will make sure that all facilities, supplies, and staff are ready on program days.

Tasks	Deadline	Persons responsible	Resources
Determine what goals can best be met through the competitive sports games. • Research the goals of the competitive sports programs. • Review the results of the needs assessment.	9/15	Jorge and Sun-Li	• Results of the needs assessment • School library • Teacher's and coach's library • Facilities and risk-management committee • Materials committee
Determine which games should be played. • Make list of sports we could play that would meet those goals. • Meet with other committees to determine the feasibility of various sports.	9/16	Jorge and Sun-Li	• Classmates • Teacher • Coaches
Create lesson plans and schedule the programs.	9/20	Jorge and Sun-Li	Scheduling and transportation committee
Make sure that the necessary equipment will be available.	9/25	Sun-Li	Materials and equipment committee
Make sure that the facilities are appropriate and that a risk-management plan is in place.	9/25	Jorge	Facilities and risk-management committee
Train other students to help with programming.	9/28	Jorge and Sun-Li William, Aki, and Laura	Teacher
Conduct the programs according to the schedule.	10/1-10/27	Jorge, Sun-Li, William, Aki, and Laura	Teacher

Create Your Action Plans

1. Each committee should create an action plan with specific items for their daily and weekly to-do lists. Use the template in table 3.5 to create your committee's action plan. If your project involves clients with disabilities, refer to the section on accessibility in step 4 (see pages 64-66). Begin your action plan by naming the committee and its members. All committee members should help create the action plan—it is essential that everyone involved in the committee have ownership in this process.
2. Review the major tasks from the checklist, and write each one in one of the left-hand columns.
3. Divide each major task into smaller tasks, assign deadlines, and decide who is responsible for each item.
4. Ask your teacher to help you develop a resource list. The resource list should include places, books, and people who can help.

Table 3.5 Action Plan Template

Committee name:

Members:

Desired outcome:

Tasks	Deadline	Persons responsible	Resources

Flow Chart Method

The final item in the planning process is the flow chart. The entire class should help prepare the flow chart because it shows how everyone's tasks fit together. If you want your project to run smoothly, you will devote a lot of time and effort to the flow chart.

The flow chart method (FCM) is a simple and thorough technique for managing the implementation of a program (Rossman 1989). It is based on the more complex program evaluation and review technique, known as PERT. PERT was developed in the 1950s for the U.S. Navy's Polaris project which had thousands of contractors who needed to coordinate their efforts (PERT 2007).

While there are several methods of charting project tasks, timelines, and critical pathways, recreation programmers have discovered that the FCM is the most practical and effective one. Once the flow chart is completed, you will have a clear picture of what must be done, how long it will take to do it, and by when it must be finished (Murphy and Howard 1977).

The most useful method for creating a flow chart was developed by Bob Rossman (1989), a veteran recreation programmer. Your checklist contains the first three items you will need for the flow chart:

1. A list of the major tasks
2. The smaller tasks that must be completed as part of each major task
3. An estimate of how long each task will take to complete

To turn your checklist into a flow chart, add these two steps:

4. Create a visual timeline that shows the weeks or months of your project.
5. Place each major task in the left column. Note the critical tasks and deadlines in the appropriate places on the timeline.

A flow chart that corresponds to the checklist in table 3.2 is shown in table 3.6.

There are several benefits to using the FCM:

- It allows you to delegate responsibility to many individuals. Everyone can see where their individual tasks fit into the overall project.
- The flow chart places tasks on a single timeline. This allows everyone to see the order in which tasks need to be completed and how some activities are dependent on others (Rossman 1989).
- When deadlines can't be met, the chart can be adjusted. One missed deadline often affects other tasks.
- It provides a valuable reference tool for next year's class if they decide to do a similar service-learning project.

A word of caution: A good flow chart does not guarantee a successful program. It is an effective communication tool and coordinating device that allows many people to work together on the same project. Remember that the flow chart is only as good as the time and effort invested in its development and the degree to which it is used during the project (Murphy and Howard 1977).

When you create your flow chart (using the activity on page 55 as a guide), you will probably need larger-than-standard paper (for example, 11 by 17 inches).

Table 3.6 Sample Flow Chart

Major function	Tasks and deadlines
Facilities and risk management (RM)	• Survey facilities (9/5). • Review RM considerations with program committees (9/8).
Programming committees	• Research and design program plans (9/15). • Meet with RM and materials committees (ongoing as needed). • Train other students to help deliver programs (9/22). • Conduct programs according to the schedule (10/2–10/27).
Scheduling and transportation	• Establish a tentative calendar (9/8). • Meet with classmates and school to confirm all dates (9/15). • Work closely with other committees, and finalize the schedule (9/20). • Confirm facilities and transportation two days before programs begin.

Major function	Tasks and deadlines
Materials	• Inventory available equipment and supplies (9/8). • Work with programming and well-being committees on materials and supplies (9/29). • Make certain that materials and supplies are ready (10/2-10/27).
Fundraising and donations	• Find out what money and donations are needed (9/15). • Solicit financial support and donations (9/29 and ongoing as needed).
Time frame	Weeks 1–2 9/4-9/15 · Weeks 3–4 9/18-9/29 · Weeks 5–6 10/2-10/13 · Weeks 7–8 10/16–10/27 · Week 9-10 10/30-11/10
Publicity	• Visit with the school's public relations offices (9/12). • Visit with local media (9/21). • Meet with news reporters (10/13–10/20).
Well-being	• Plan for snacks, icebreakers, and social events (9/15). • Work with materials and fundraising committees to get needed items (9/27). • Deliver snacks, icebreakers, etc., as scheduled (10/2–10/27). • Plan an end-of-project celebration (10/27).
Evaluation	• Develop an evaluation (10/13). • Conduct the evaluation (10/25). • Analyze the results and write a report (11/3).
Student project Leader	• Call class meetings for committee updates (ongoing). • Keep track of committees' progress (ongoing). • Involve others in troubleshooting problems (ongoing). • Act as communications liaison between students, teacher, and clients (ongoing).

Create Your Flow Chart

Even if they are not completed, gather your checklist and action plans, and modify them as you work on the flow chart.

1. Consider the total time frame of your project, and divide the timeline into blocks. For example, if your project takes place over a 14-day period, you need to itemize each day on the timeline. If the project takes longer than 14 days, you may want to use 1- or 2-week blocks. If the project extends over 10 months, you will want to use 1-month time blocks.
2. List your major tasks in the left-hand column.
3. Fill in the major tasks and deadlines.
4. Make careful note of where the work of one major task depends on the product of another major task. For example, equipment cannot be purchased until funds are available from the fundraising committee.
5. Keep your flow chart where the entire class can review it throughout the duration of the project. If you can, post it in your classroom. If this isn't possible, roll the flow chart up and store it in a poster tube. You can tape it on the wall on the days the class needs it. There may be a bulletin board you can use to display the mission and other information about your project. If the flow chart can be reduced to an 8.5-by-11-inch page, consider giving a copy to each student. Also, if you have a scanner (or copier with scanning capability) available, you can scan the flow chart into a pdf file that can be posted on a Web site if you have one.

SUMMARY

Congratulations! Your planning process is now complete, and you and your classmates are prepared for action. Since life has a way of interfering with the best-laid plans, don't be surprised if you have to modify deadlines, functions, and tasks along the way. Look to your teacher for advice if you find yourselves in a difficult spot.

REFERENCES

Campbell, D. 1974. *If you don't know where you're going, you'll probably end up somewhere else*. Allen, TX: Thomas More.

Clark, D. 2007. Learning domains or Bloom's taxonomy. www.nwlink.com/~donclark/hrd/bloom.html.

Mager, R.F. 1997. *Preparing instructional objectives: A critical tool in the development of effective instruction*. (3rd ed). Atlanta: CEP Press.

Murphy, J., and D. Howard. 1977. *Delivery of community leisure services: An holistic approach*. Philadelphia: Lea and Febiger.

PERT. 2007. Retrieved from NETMBA Business Knowledge Center: www.NetMBA.com/operations/project/pert/.

Radtke, J.M. 1998. *Strategic communications for nonprofit organizations: Seven steps to creating a successful plan*. Indianapolis: Wiley.

Rossman, J.R. 1989. *Recreation programming: Designing leisure experiences*. Champaign, IL: Sagamore.

Russell, R.V. 1982. *Planning programs in recreation*. St. Louis: Mosby.

REFLECTION

Your teacher may have you reflect on the planning process by writing in your journal. Step 1 discussed structured journaling. The following three questions can be modified for your situation. To write a structured journal entry, respond to the questions, in sequence, from three perspectives—yours, the team's, and the project's.

1. What happened? (Describe what happened to you, to the team, with the project.).
2. So what? (Describe what effect those events had on you, on others, and on the project. What did you observe that led you to believe this?)
3. Now what? (Based on questions 1 and 2, how can you apply what you've learned to your project?)

This journaling exercise will help you understand that planning is a formative process. Sometimes the questions we ask are more important than the answers. You are now thinking ahead, you have plans, and you will be flexible and responsive when people, places, and events don't meet your expectations. Also, remember that there is a checklist at the end of step 2 that will direct you to helpful activities should problems arise.

STUDENT CHECKLIST

- ☐ The mission statement and goals have been completed and agreed to by the entire class.
- ☐ The checklist for the major tasks is completed.
- ☐ The major tasks have been assigned to student committees.
- ☐ The student committees have completed action plans for their major task(s).
- ☐ The flow chart has been completed.
- ☐ The checklist, action plans, and flow chart are in a central location where everyone has access to them.

STEP

Implementing the Plan

Step 5
Finishing the Project

Step 4
Implementing the Plan

Step 3
Planning the Project

Step 2
Building an Effective Team

Step 1
Launching the Project

In this step you will

- **manage your time and complete tasks,**
- **apply group-process skills,**
- **deliver quality customer service, and**
- **evaluate your project.**

> **Planning is bringing the future into the present so that you can do something about it now.**
>
> *—Alan Lakein*

You've now completed your planning, and you understand what your project is supposed to do and how your class will do the work. Alan Lakein's statement applies to how planning (step 3) relates to implementation (step 4). As your class planned its project, you whittled the big picture down to specific details.

Now, as you move into implementation, recognize that you have little (if any) control over people, places, and things. Not everything will unfold as you have planned. It is important now for everyone to work well as part of the team. Keep in mind the big picture of the project as you do your individual work. How will you and your classmates remain flexible and responsive to changing conditions? You will need regular and clear communication, cooperation, and coordination.

Step 4 describes techniques to help you manage your time and complete your tasks, as well as ideas to facilitate teamwork and communication. In addition, this chapter discusses customer service, accessibility, and how to evaluate your service-learning project. Customer service is an essential skill. It is also important to make your project as accessible as possible so that everyone can participate regardless of ability. Finally, clients will need to evaluate your project before it ends. Hence, instructions for designing and implementing a simple evaluation are included.

MANAGING TIME AND COMPLETING TASKS

The following two suggestions will help you and your classmates finish your work on time. First, you are not expected to be an expert, so doesn't hesitate to ask for help and clarification when you need it. There are no stupid questions. In fact, asking for help is a mark of professionalism.

Second, if you don't have anything to do at the moment, help someone else. A student or employee who is behaving professionally does not stand around waiting to be told what to do. She asks where help is needed and she pitches in. Several other actions can help keep you on task.

Reflect on Mission, Goals, and Learning Objectives

You had an orientation to learning objectives in step 1, and your class wrote detailed goals and objectives for your service-learning project during the planning stage in step 3. Now is a good time to review your mission statement, learning goals, and objectives. They are the road map for your project. Make sure everyone has access to these documents by posting them in the classroom, or by providing everyone a copy that they can keep in the front of their project folder. If students seem to be losing their focus, it may be a good idea to add a review of mission, goals, and objectives to a class meeting agenda.

Use Your Action Plans and Flow Chart

Your action plans list the details of who needs to do what and by when. It may be helpful if each committee selects a leader to help keep everyone else on track. Items for the leader to check include the following:

- Does each student have a copy of the group's action plan?
- Does each student have a daily planner?
- Has each student written the task deadlines in his or her planner?
- When do students need reminders and checkpoints?
- How do people like to be reminded (for example, by phone call, e-mail, text message, or instant message)?
- Does everyone have the resources they need to accomplish their tasks? Perhaps they need, for instance, money or referral information for people they should contact.

Remember, the main reason students don't finish tasks is that they are not sure of what to do or how to do it, or perhaps they don't understand how important a deadline is. The flow chart is

Photos and Videos

You will want to have records of what the students and clients are doing throughout the project. If your school has a photographer, set up appointments for the photographer to take pictures or videos. If your school doesn't have a photographer, choose an interested student or students for the task. It's a good idea to take pictures of the preparations and of the work in progress so that future students can see the process unfold. Of course, you'll want to have pictures and videos of the event itself. These can be used for celebration, publicity, or sharing. Pictures can be tacked to a bulletin board, or the pictures and video can be posted on a Web site. If photos are to be published, the people in the photos will need to sign a photo-release form before you print their picture in any public medium. An example photo-release form is shown in figure 4.1.

I hereby give ______________________ the absolute right and permission to
(name of school)

copyright and/or publish the photographic portraits or pictures of ______________________.
(name of person)

I agree that the photograph becomes the exclusive property of ______________________ and I waive all rights hereto.
(the school)

I waive all rights to inspect and/or approve copy that may be used in conjunction with the photograph and the use to which it may be applied.

The photograph—whole, in part, or composite—may be used as the school sees fit in the publication of educational materials, and the advertising thereof, and for any other lawful purposes.

____
Date

____
Model (if the model is a minor, the parent or guardian signs)

____
____
____
Address

____
Phone number

Figure 4.1 Sample photo-release form.

another important tool for showing everyone how important their smaller tasks and deadlines are to the project as a whole. Post your flow chart and modify it as necessary.

The class will need to pay close attention to teamwork. If you pay close attention to how the team functions, things will probably go smoothly. If you neglect group process, the project may falter. The suggestions in the following section will help your team work well together.

APPLYING GROUP-PROCESS SKILLS

In a best-case scenario, you and your classmates will have already completed the activities in step 2 and you will have built an effective team. It's more likely, though, that you have too much to do in too little time and that you might need to revisit some of the activities and techniques that were covered in step 2. The team-building checklist (page 37) can help you decide whether your team could use some fine-tuning.

Are You Working as a Team?

A team is a group of individuals working together toward a common goal. The checklist states, "If some students appear unmotivated, use active listening to find out whether they are uncertain of what to do or whether they are uninterested in the project, or both. If you can figure out what is missing, such as direction, skills, or commitment, try applying the suggestions in the team development and leadership model that you learned about during step 2.

A review of the team-development and leadership model in step 2 will help your team identify the source of its problems. If students lack direction, check their task sheets. Are they complete and detailed enough? Does everyone understand what they are supposed to do? Do they have the skills and resources they need? As you coach each other through the process of completing your tasks, it may be helpful to regularly check in with each other to exchange feedback. Ask your teacher to take part in these discussions. He or she can help you get the support and resources you need.

If some of the students are not interested in the project, your class has a more difficult problem. A heart-to-heart discussion about what can be done to increase their commitment may be in order. If the class worked together to choose a meaningful project and if it then co-created a strong mission statement, all the students should feel a sense of ownership. In some cases, trading tasks can help students capitalize on their strengths and increase motivation.

Fine-Tuning Communication

All teams need good communication and conflict-resolution skills. If people are not communicating well, try the Practicing Communication Skills activity in step 2 (page 23), and review the material on active listening, giving and receiving feedback, and giving compliments.

Every student can help create a positive atmosphere by catching people doing things right. Catching people doing things right means that the students and the teacher give lots of compliments when students do things well. It has been stated that it takes four compliments to outweigh one criticism. You can help shift a person's attention away from criticism and toward the positive by giving lots of genuine encouragement. It may help to post a sign that says, "Catch people doing things right: Give a compliment today!"

It's also important for everyone to feel comfortable giving and receiving constructive criticism. Without it, people tend not to talk about issues that are bothering them. As a result, they might lash out in unconstructive ways. You may want to consider posting another sign that says, "Please tell me *kindly* if I'm doing something wrong. Tell me *now* so that I can fix it. Don't wait until tomorrow."

Open communication, compliments, and regular, constructive feedback will help prevent serious conflicts. In the event that two or more students get into a serious conflict, it might be helpful for students to speak with the teacher together. The teacher can listen to both sides and serve as a mediator. Don't let problems build; seek assistance before a small problem becomes a big one.

Keep in Touch With Each Other

Students need to maintain communication with each other and with the teacher. Consider using an electronic medium for this task. Several electronic media—such as electronic bulletin boards, instant messages, text messages, and e-mail—allow students to make regular postings, ask questions, or ask for help.

Electronic communication, however, has its limitations. It will not work well unless everyone has easy access to a computer, and nothing replaces face-to-face communication when someone has a problem. When you speak to someone directly, you can see his or her facial expressions and body language. It is helpful to meet periodically, perhaps once a week or so, for a class discussion that all the students would attend. Each task group would give an update on their part of the project. The teacher and/or student project leader could adjust the flow chart during the meeting if necessary. These meetings can also serve as reminders to everyone that the rest of the group is counting on them to complete their work on time.

Formative Feedback

Formative feedback is input that you receive while you are still in the process of working on a task rather than waiting until it is finished. It's especially important to seek feedback in the beginning or middle stages and not to wait until the task is completely finished. Once a task has been completed, it's difficult for someone to give you guidance. Critical feedback that is given after a task is completed tends to result in hurt feelings and anger because people feel like their work was not appreciated. In management, this is called the leave alone, zap approach. An example of leave alone, zap management is when a manager or teacher says something vague, such as, "Go make posters." You, the employee or student, buy the poster boards, decide what to write, and prepare the posters. You spend hours getting the posters just right. You show them to your teacher and she says, "The posters can't be pink!" Since pink is your favorite color, you used pink poster board. What should you do? This situation could have been avoided through formative feedback along the way. Here's how:

- Always remember that the person who is asking you to do something, whether it's your teacher or one of your classmates, probably has an idea of what he or she wants. This person often doesn't have the time, however, or know how to explain the details. You can help that person and yourself by consistently asking for their input as the task progresses.
- As you proceed with planning and implementation, ask questions: "What colors did you have in mind? How much may I spend on supplies? How do you want this to look?"
- Once you've decided on what your posters should say or on what your marketing plan should look like, bring those ideas to the teacher or to your classmates and ask for their input.

By asking for input, you are taking the initiative. You are keeping the lines of communication open by asking others for their input while the project is coming together. You can therefore make changes as you go. The result is a product that pleases everyone. Things are accomplished in ways that satisfy everyone.

Dealing With Drama

Do you remember the ground rules you set in step 2? If cliques seem to be forming or if it feels like there is too much drama surrounding the project, it may be time to revisit the rules. The following list is a revised version of the advice from step 2. It describes how to use your ground rules now that you are heavily involved in project tasks.

1. Make sure the ground rules are visible and available to each student. Consider reading them at the start of each class meeting, posting them in the classroom, or keeping them in the front of your notebook.
2. Continue to challenge each other on the ground rules. Ask your teacher to challenge you on them too. If you did not set a tone of strict adherence to the rules early in the process, you may need to talk about them as a group again.
3. If one or more ground rules apply to a particular situation, bring them to the group's attention. For example, if you are about to conduct a meeting, you might remind everyone about the group's commitment to active listening and to "I" statements.
4. If a ground rule is consistently being broken, have a class discussion about what should be done. Ask your teacher to assist with this process.

In a sense, all the ground rules are about respect.

5. If time allows, ask the class whether it would like to make changes to the ground rules.

In a sense all of the ground rules are about respect. The golden rule, "Do unto others as you would have them do unto you," is a time-tested principle that will serve you well should you have any doubts about how to treat others. Not one of us is perfect, and the best we can do is to have positive intentions about the project, classmates, and clients. The only person you can control is yourself, so commit to doing the best you can.

Running Efficient Meetings

If meetings seem to be a waste of time or if tasks are not progressing as planned, review and implement the guidelines for conducting effective and efficient meetings. The following are suggestions for addressing common meeting problems:

- If your class meetings are inefficient, try establishing time limits on your agenda. If your classmates want to have long discussions that go nowhere, call a vote to decide whether the agenda should be changed. Usually people are relieved to move forward with the agenda.
- If students bog down in lengthy discussions without taking action, consider changing the agenda to an action-items-only agenda. Deal only with items for which action can be taken. Avoid items that can only be talked about. For example, your action-item agenda item might state, "Select one of three T-shirt designs" instead of "Brainstorm ideas for t-shirt designs."
- If students have too many details to share in too little time, consider setting up an electronic discussion or bulletin board where students can report progress and ask for help. Teachers tend to work from morning to afternoon, but students often do much of their work in the evening. An electronic chat room or bulletin board can help the class resolve issues outside of class. This will help the actual class meetings run better.

Solving Problems

"Life is what happens while you we're making other plans." This means that things never seem to occur as we expect them to. Problems arise. Most problems are small and can be resolved by having a few students work together or by consulting the teacher. When complex problems arise, consider applying the problem-solving and decision-making strategies, as well as the brainstorming techniques, covered in step 3. It is especially important to involve the entire class when everyone needs to feel ownership of the solution—that is, everyone should understand the problem, agree on how to fix it, and be committed to the solution.

There is a vital thing to know about getting a group to buy in to a solution. You, the leader, might have a pretty good idea about how to solve a problem. If you tell the group, "Here's the problem, and this is what I think we should do," you may encounter resistance. But if you present the problem to the group and then step back as they brainstorm and work through it, they are likely to think of the same solution you did—*it is not wasted time*. On the contrary, the group will feel that they own the problem. They will buy in to the solution. The group will now want to implement the solution rather than sabotage it. When it was *your* problem, they didn't own it, nor did they own the solution because they didn't think of the solution on their own. It is rarely a waste of time to let the group solve a complex problem.

Using Reflection to Your Advantage: The Model Manager

Here is a creative reflection exercise for your class. Have each student reflect on and discuss what an ideal manager of your service-learning project would do.

Create a job description for an ideal manager who could get the most out of your team. Have each student answer the following questions:

1. What is working well for me and for our team?
2. What is not working well for me and for our team?
3. If I could change one thing today, what would it be?
4. If I could keep one thing the same, what would it be?

Another common problem is unprofessional behavior from certain students. This is to be expected because many students have not been in situations where they have been expected to behave like professionals. If there are students in your class who are not acting in a professional manner, revisit the Showing Professionalism self-evaluation in chapter 3. Ask each person to rate his or her professional behavior. Next, ask each student to set a behavioral goal for the remainder of the project. Discuss with the group how they can help each other exhibit professional behavior.

It is time to cover three more elements of successful project implementation: customer service, accessibility, and project evaluation.

As a group, discuss your answers and write a job description for an ideal team manager. Then consider how you are all team managers, and discuss how each of you can take personal responsibility to make these things happen. Remember, there is no *I* in *team*. All of you will have to work together if your project is to be successful.

CUSTOMER SERVICE

When your project involves providing services directly to people, you have customers. The term *customer* can be used interchangeably with *client*, and it typically refers to a person who buys your goods or services. Even though nonprofit organizations provide goods and services for free, their customers still have a right to expect high-quality customer service.

You, the students, may not view yourselves as professionals, but your clients will expect professionalism and good service anyway. It might be tempting to think, *But we are just students. That's not our job.* In reality, though, it *is* your job to be available, professional, caring, and helpful. If you want to make your project excellent in every way, you must provide good customer service. The following guidelines explain the basics of high-quality customer service.

Customer-Service Guidelines

To deliver good customer service, the students must have positive attitudes. Students should follow these principles:

- Be available. Ensure that clients know how and when they can reach you, and make sure there are enough staff members to handle inquiries. Be able to answer phone calls, respond to e-mail messages, or answer Internet inquiries.
- Be accurate. Make sure every student has easy access to accurate information on directions, costs, services, and so on. This information should be attractively displayed to the clients, whether on poster board, on a Web site, or in another format.
- Be positive. Decide in advance that you will be courteous, helpful, and polite to the clients—especially to the ones with complaints. View every problem or complaint as a positive situation rather than as a negative one. The client has given you an opportunity to make things better. Your response should be this: "I'm so glad you are telling us this because we want to fix this problem."
- Be helpful. Take extra steps to give people what they need. If a person asks for directions, walk him or her to where they want to go. Avoid saying, "I can't help you with that," or "That's not my job." Instead find out what the client needs. If you can't help her, tell her that you'll find the answer and that you'll call her back by a certain time. If someone else will call her, make sure she knows the name of the person who will contact her and when she can expect the call.
- Be committed. Always follow through on the commitments you make to clients and to each other. Even if you don't have a solution or if you weren't able to finish a task, you need to follow through. Make sure you do what you said you would, and follow through in every case. Following through promptly will result in people's regarding you as someone who can be counted on to keep his word and get things done.

Communication in Customer Service

Good customer service requires good communication. Review the active listening and assertive communication guidelines from step 2. These basic communication skills will help you treat clients the way they should be treated. Additional suggestions for what you should say and what you

Table 4.1 Language to Build Cooperative Relationships With Your Clients

Cooperation-Building Phrases	Fight-Starting Phrases
Make a request	**Not a demand**
• Will you . . . please. • If you will . . . then I can . . . • It works well when . . . • The rate is . . . • Would you mind waiting while I . . .	• You have to . . . , You must . . . • You should . . . • It's required that you . . . • It will cost you . . . • Wait here . . .
Show that you are willing to help.	**Don't be unwilling to help.**
• Let me see what I can do to help. • I'll find out and get back to you. • I want to help find a solution. • Let's see what we can work out.	• It's not my job. • I don't know. • We can't do that. • You sure have a problem.
Be precise	**Not indefinite**
• I'm going to . . . • I'll do this much . . .	• I'll try . . . (When you say you will try, the person assumes you *will* try.)
Effective language gets results	**Ineffective language blocks**
• *How* can I help you? (Note: open-ended question helps you gather information about what they need.)	• *May* I help you? (Asks permission. This closed question limits the information you get from them.)
Use the word "and" to give credibility to what you say.	**Avoid the word "but" because it negates everything you say before it.**
• Thanks for completing the registration form, *and* . . . (makes them ready to do what you request)	• The registration form is completed, *but* . . . (makes them ready to argue)
Be supportive	**Not blaming**
• There are a few more areas on the form you will need to complete . . .	• You didn't do this right.
Give an explanation, avoid policy	**The word "policy" sets people on edge**
• For the safety of everyone, it is necessary for you to . . .	• Our policy requires you to . . .

should not say to clients are given in table 4.1. These scripted statements provide you with language that encourages a cooperative relationship with each customer instead of a combative one.

The wording suggestions in table 4.1 will help ensure smooth, cooperative communication. The activity on page 65 will help you apply these skills to scenarios you might encounter.

ACCESSIBILITY

You need to make sure that your service-learning events are accessible to everyone. With the passage of the Americans with Disabilities Act (ADA) in 1990, all event planners are now obligated to make their meeting locations accessible to persons with disabilities.

Before the Event

There are several tasks that you must attend to as you plan.

- Ask the people who will attend whether they have any needs that you can address that will in turn allow them to participate fully in the activities. This can be done through the registration process. On the registration form, provide a space for people to note their special needs. Then contact them to make arrangements.

Watch Your Words

The words you choose at the beginning of a conversation set the tone, so make sure your words show your willingness to help find solutions. Consider how and why you should respond differently in each of these four situations. Use the suggestions in table 4.1 to check and revise your answers.

1. Client: "How can I get hold of your teacher?"
   Student: "Call him."

Why wouldn't you say this to a client?______________________________

____

How would you rephrase this response? ______________________________

____

2. Client: "Is there anyone who can help me?"
   Student: "I don't think so."

Why wouldn't you say this to a client?______________________________

How would you rephrase this response? ______________________________

3. Client: "Can you get my parking pass by 2:00 p.m. today?"
   Student: "I'll try."

Why wouldn't you say this to a client?______________________________

How would you rephrase this response? ______________________________

4. Student to client: "You have to pay $75."

Why wouldn't you say this to a client?______________________________

How would you rephrase this request? ______________________________

Customer service is a fundamental skill that you will use in almost every job you ever do. If you are new to customer service, some of the language may feel awkward at first, but as you employ these suggestions, you will feel more comfortable helping clients. You will start to relax and have fun.

- Include a statement on your publicity materials such as "Our school seeks to fully comply with the Americans with Disabilities Act (ADA). Anyone who needs accommodations based on a disability may request support and assistance. Please contact us directly at (phone number and e-mail address) at least two weeks in advance so that we can accommodate your needs."
- Considering appointing someone to be a disability services coordinator.
- Walk through the site where your service-learning activities will take place. You may find it helpful to review the Americans with Disabilities Act www.usdoj.gov/crt/ada/adahom1.htm as well as the free, detailed facility checklist at www.ga.wa.gov/ada/instlist.htm. Things to check for include the following:
  - Equipment, such as elevators, on site to accommodate persons with disabilities

- Accessible restrooms for both men and women
- Accessible telephones
- Accessible parking
- Accessible eating areas, including Braille menus if people will be in a restaurant
- Accessible transportation
- Emergency evacuation procedures, such as using flashing lights to alert deaf and hearing-impaired people that they need to evacuate the building
- Grassy area for guide dogs to use during the day

- When the people with special needs arrive, meet them at a designated location so that you can explain the arrangements that have been made to accommodate them.

Special Considerations

If you need to make provisions for people with hearing impairments, visual impairments, or learning disabilities, you may need to ask for assistance from your school's disability support services office.

Issues to consider include the following:

- Are sign-language interpreters or listening-amplification equipment needed?
- If guides for those with visual impairments are needed, train them in advance.
- Do you have readers or note takers for people with learning disabilities?
- If participants are likely to have diabetes, lung disease, heart conditions, asthma, or arthritis, you should provide both a place and time for them to rest periodically.

During the Event

If many participants with disabilities will attend your event, make sure you have arranged for students to provide one-on-one assistance. You may need to recruit some volunteers just for this purpose if you and your classmates will be busy with other aspects of the event.

- Have someone meet each participant with special needs in order to make sure that all his or her accommodation needs have been met.
- Provide special seating for people with seeing or hearing difficulties.
- Have a volunteer who is prepared to read or to fill out forms for someone with a visual impairment or for someone who is unable to read for any reason.

It is critical to establish a point of communication with your clients and participants ahead of your events. Provide a way for those with disabilities to inform you of their needs in advance so that you can make preparations. By asking for information and offering to assist, you will be telling the community that your events are inclusive. This will help people with disabilities feel comfortable attending your event.

EVALUATING YOUR PROJECT

To evaluate your project, you should collect some information soon after it ends. You should do the following: Gather information for a service-hour report, and design a short client satisfaction evaluation so that you can get feedback about the project.

The evaluation helps you document what happened, find out what you did well, and determine where improvements can be made. The service-hour report is a good way to collect and report information about the quantity of service provided. The quality of service is important too. Your clients can tell you a lot about the quality of your project and about how much it helped them. A client satisfaction evaluation will allow your clients to tell you what they think went well and what did not go well so that you can make improvements. Your clients probably won't want to spend a lot of time completing surveys, so your satisfaction evaluation should be focused, short, and easy to complete. A typical evaluation contains 5 to 10 easy-to-answer questions, where clients can circle their responses, combined with one or two open-ended questions, where clients can write down their thoughts and opinions. In addition to keeping the evaluation short, ask questions in a way that makes the information you gather useful.

Service-Hour Reports

You will want to gather information about attendance and staffing before your service-learning event (or events) has concluded. You will use a slightly different format depending on whether your service-learning project is a one-time event or whether it will be repeated. Here are some items to record during the event so that you can prepare a service-hour report.

- Name of activity, program, or event
- Location and time
- Attendance
- Number of people registered (this is relevant only if your event required registration)
- Hours of operation (how long the event lasted; repeat this for the number of times your event occurred)
- Staff hours (count student hours, teacher hours, and volunteer hours separately)

Programming experts Bob Rossman and Barbara Schlatter provide two models for service-hour reports. The report format varies a little depending on whether your project was a one-time event or whether it was repeated. An example of an event-report format is shown in figure 4.2, and a program report format is shown in figure 4.3.

The reporting format for events that is illustrated in figure 4.2 introduces three concepts: service hours, staff hours, and an efficiency ratio. Service hours are calculated by multiplying the attendance at the event times the number of hours the event was going. For example, if 225 participants attended a 4-hour health fair, the service hours would be 225 multiplied by 4, or 900 hours. Staff hours are calculated by multiplying

Service-Learning Event Name ____________________

Location ____________________

Date ____________________ Time ____________________

A. Registration
B. Attendance (how many people came)
C. Service hours (attendance multiplied by the hours of event operation)
D. Staff hours (number of staff multiplied by the hours of operation)
E. Efficiency ratio (service hours divided by staff hours)

Figure 4.2 Service-learning event report format.
Adapted from Rossman and Schlatter 2000.

Service-Learning Program Name ____________________

Location ____________________

Date ____________________ Time ____________________

A. Registration
B. Number of sessions
C. Length of each program
D. Hours of program operation (number of sessions multiplied by the length of each program)
E. Total attendance (how many people came to all the programs)
F. Average attendance (total attendance divided by the hours of program operation)
G. Service hours (number of staff multiplied by the hours of program operation)
H. Total staff hours
I. Efficiency ratio (service hours divided by staff hours)

Figure 4.3 Service-learning report format for repeating programs.
Adapted from Rossman and Schlatter 2000.

the number of staff members working (student hours + teacher's hours + volunteer hours) times the number of hours of the event. For example, if 35 staff worked for 4 hours at a health fair, the staff hours would equal 35 multiplied by 4, or 140 hours. The efficiency ratio provides a statistic that can be used to compare the efficiency of service-learning programs. The efficiency ratio is calculated by dividing the number of service hours by the number of staff hours. In the example provided, the 900 service hours would be divided by 140 staff hours for an efficiency ratio of 6.4.

The reporting format for repeating programs is illustrated in figure 4.3. It introduces five new concepts in addition to the ones already covered. First, you will want to determine hours of program operation by multiplying the number of sessions by the length of time of each session. For example, three sessions lasting three hours each would equal nine hours of program operation. Total attendance is calculated by taking the attendance at each event and adding it together. For example, if 12 people came to the first session, 25 to the second, and 15 to the third, your total attendance would be 12 + 25 + 15, which equals 52. The average attendance would be 52/3, which equals approximately 17. The service hours are thus the total attendance times the length of each program. For example, 52 in total attendance times 3 program hours equals 156 service hours. The staff hours are the number of staff members working each event times the hours of total program operation. For

---

Thank you for coming to our Make Our Community Green environmental health cleanup event. Please take a few minutes to answer some questions that will help us improve the program.

How many people came with you? ________ children ________ adults

For how long did you attend the event? (circle one)

30 minutes 1 hour 1 hour 30 minutes 2 hours

How satisfied were you with the Make Our Community Green program? (circle one)

1 = very dissatisfied
2 = dissatisfied
3 = somewhat dissatisfied
4 = in the middle, neither satisfied nor dissatisfied
5 = somewhat satisfied
6 = satisfied
7 = very satisfied

Rate your satisfaction with the following:

	Very dissatisfied						Very satisfied
1. Children's games	1	2	3	4	5	6	7
2. Recycling tips and tools	1	2	3	4	5	6	7
3. Dealing With Pests Around the House booth	1	2	3	4	5	6	7
4. Energy Conservation booth	1	2	3	4	5	6	7
5. Get Involved in Positive Change booth	1	2	3	4	5	6	7
6. Information you can use at home	1	2	3	4	5	6	7

What did you like best about the program? ________________________________

____

What is one thing we can do to improve the program? ________________________________

____

Thank you for coming to our event and sharing your opinion.

Figure 4.4 Service-learning client satisfaction survey.

example, if 10 staff members worked each of the 3-hour events (9 total program hours), the staff hours would be 90, or 10 times 9. Therefore, your efficiency ratio for these individual programs is 156 service hours divided by 90 staff hours for an efficiency ratio of 1.7.

All service-learning projects should complete a program evaluation report similar to those described earlier. The information in the report provides a record of the quantity of service your class has delivered. In addition to quantity of service, you'll want to know something about the quality of the project. To determine the quality of your project, you will need to ask the clients.

Client Satisfaction Surveys

Before your clients leave the project site, you should have their written evaluations of the project. The satisfaction evaluation determines whether the clients thought the program was a good one. Client-reported satisfaction is a measure that you, your teachers, and your school can use to evaluate the quality of the project. This information will be useful for future projects and possibly for securing funding from grants or community agencies. Your goal is to design a short, appealing, straight-to-the-point evaluation for your clients to complete.

Before you begin designing your evaluation, review appendix A. It contains detailed, useful information that will help you design your questions, collect data, analyze results, and write a report. Your client satisfaction survey will likely begin with several demographic questions and will be followed by client satisfaction questions. A typical evaluation concludes with one or two open-ended questions that are meant to gather information about what worked well and what could be improved.

An example client satisfaction survey is shown in figure 4.4. There are many questions you can ask depending on the nature of your service-learning project. Examples of question topics are covered in figure 4.5.

Your project may have a combination of goals pertaining to, for example, knowledge, social interaction, service, fun, and environment. As you review these areas, remember that you should ask only the most important questions. Clients won't want to spend a lot of time filling out a survey, so a satisfaction survey should never be longer than one page. Whatever your survey design, test it before you give it to your clients, as described

Knowledge and Skills

I learned more about diet and nutrition.

I learned more about healthy exercise.

I learned more about children's activities.

I increased my skills in ____________.

I increased my knowledge about ____________.

I changed my attitude about ____________.

Social

I made connections with new people.

I enjoyed the companionship.

I enjoyed being with my friends.

I made new friends who I will see in the future.

This is something our family can do together.

Services

I increased my knowledge of, my access to, or my use of services.

I increased my ability to solve life's problems.

I increased my ability to use available services.

I increased my ability to care for my children and parents.

This program helped me meet my emergency needs.

What I learned will help decrease my emotional trauma.

I increased my desire and ability to help others.

I increased my safety and feelings of security.

Fun and Quality of Life

I had fun at this program.

I improved my quality of life.

I improved the quality of life for my family.

I increased my pride in my neighborhood.

I increased my sense of community.

Environment

The area was fresh and clean.

I liked the open space.

I felt safe when I was here.

Everything was easy to find and get to.

Adapted from Corporation for National Service; Rossman and Schlatter 2000.

Figure 4.5 Client satisfaction survey topics.

in appendix A. Devise a strategy to get as many people as possible to fill it out. For example, if you have a door where clients enter and exit, station a couple of students there to ask people questions as they leave the program.

SUMMARY

Project implementation is the most time-consuming part of your service-learning project. It has the potential to be the most exciting, most informative, and most frustrating portion of the project. Using the tips and tools in this chapter, you can maximize the involvement of every student and make the service-learning project a pleasant experience for everyone. Be excited that you and your classmates are doing something worthwhile and that the lessons you learn will last a lifetime. Service-learning projects can require a lot of work, but you will get out of it what you put into it.

REFERENCES

Corporation for National Service. Toolkit: A user's guide to evaluation for national service programs. http://nationalserviceresources.org/resources/online_pubs/perf_meas/usersguide.php.

Estes, C.A. 1998. *Student handbook for the annual Cortland recreation conference*. Cortland, NY: SUNY.

Greenaway, R. 2004. Big picture reviewing: Seeing the woods as well as the trees. http://reviewing.co.uk/articles/big-picture-reviewing.htm.

Rossman, J.R., and B.E. Schlatter. 2000. *Recreation programming: Designing leisure experiences* (3rd ed). Champaign, IL: Sagamore.

State University of New York. n.d. Making meetings and conferences accessible. www.cortland.edu/hr/making%20meeting%20accessible.pdf.

REFLECTION

You are not yet finished with your project. Your teacher probably assigned you to make regular journal entries (refer to journaling in step 1). Now you will complete the final phase of reflection and evaluation. Step 5 contains your final activities and brings closure to your service-learning experience.

STUDENT CHECKLIST

- ☐ All students know the mission, goals, and learning objectives.
- ☐ Students are managing their time well.
- ☐ Students are reporting necessary information back to the group.
- ☐ Students are receiving formative feedback on their parts of the project.
- ☐ Someone is designated to take photos and/or videos of every phase of the project.
- ☐ The team is functioning well. If problems arise, the team revisits the activities in chapter 3.
- ☐ A sign was posted that encourages both compliments and constructive criticism.
- ☐ All students know how to provide good customer service.
- ☐ Steps have been taken to make the events accessible to people with special needs.
- ☐ Students are ready to record the information for a service-hour report.
- ☐ A client satisfaction evaluation has been designed, and data collection is underway.

STEP 5

Finishing the Project

In this step you will

- **celebrate your accomplishments,**
- **reflect on what you have learned, and**
- **prepare reports and records.**

> **We do not learn from our experiences;**
> **we learn from processing our experiences.**
>
> *—John Dewey*

Now that your service-learning project is nearly finished, it is time to reflect on what you've learned. Reflection will help you maximize the benefits of your hard work. You have learned many new skills (human relations skills, project management skills), and you have learned about your community and the value of service. Through celebration, reflection, and evaluation, you now have the opportunity to synthesize what you have learned. You are probably ready for the project to end, but consider the potential benefits that celebration, reflection, and evaluation can hold for you (Reed and Koliba n.d.):

- Career exploration and networking
- Leadership development
- Knowledge
- Spiritual fulfillment
- Professional development
- Political consciousness

Here are some ways that you can facilitate your reflection process and maximize your benefits.

CELEBRATION

It's time to celebrate your accomplishments with your fellow students, volunteers, and clients. Celebration has several benefits. Celebration provides closure—to end your experience without closure leaves everyone with an impression that something was missing. Saying thank you and goodbye is a natural and important part of a project cycle. Your celebration activities are also opportunities to stimulate reflection and to gather information about the community's needs and about its desires for future projects. Your celebration can be informal or formal, and it can be anything from a casual meal at a restaurant or a potluck dinner to an event with a structured program that highlights what students have learned. Review the sections that follow for ideas on presenting skits, photo essays, songs, slide shows, art, or poetry during your celebration. When you incorporate reflection activities in your celebration, it recognizes and celebrates everyone's contributions and it facilitates reflection. The students, teacher, and clients should decide what type of celebration will meet your needs. The following are ideas for celebrations:

- Sharing a meal
- Recognition event
- Planning a recreational activity

You can also celebrate your accomplishments by spreading the word about your project. The following are ways to get the word out:

- Write an article for a local newspaper.

© Mark Rose/iStockphoto

Sharing a recreational activity is a great way to celebrate a group's success.

- Put a display or bulletin board in a school or other public area, such as the library.
- Post information on the school's Web site, or send it to other service-learning Web sites such as www.compact.org (see the section titled News in the Media and Latest News of Interest).

In addition to celebrating, you should personally reflect on the project. Your teacher will probably have you complete some reflection exercises. The following section discusses these assignments.

REFLECTION

It is often said that hindsight is 20/20. You can learn a lot about your project by reflecting on what you've learned. Reflecting is simply thinking critically about your service-learning experience. It is normal to assume that you have already learned what you are going to learn from the project and that additional reflection exercises are unnecessary. Nothing could be further from the truth. Donald Shon, in his book *The Reflective Practitioner: How Professionals Think in Action* (1983), calls on professionals to better understand their actions by thinking about them. Of course we think about our actions all the time. Structured reflection, however, is different from ordinary thinking because it helps us make a habit of thinking about thinking. Shon notes that when practice becomes repetitive (or when we are in a hurry), we miss important opportunities to think about what we are doing. The selective attention we develop causes us to miss valuable insights (as cited by Reed and Koliba n.d.). In terms of your project, thinking about thinking is especially important for students to do. Each student has worked on various aspects of the project and has not yet reflected on the project as a whole.

You and your classmates reflected on the project as you worked through it. For example, writing in your journal, conducting client-needs assessments and contracting, writing your mission statement and goals, using the Self-Evaluation of Professionalism (table 2.3), and conducting meetings were all opportunities for reflection. Now that your project is complete, it is time for each student to reflect on what he or she has accomplished and learned. Five reflection formats are discussed here: final journal, reflection paper, program and self-evaluation, portfolio, or presentation.

One of these options may appeal to you more than the others depending on your learning style. Also consider less traditional, creative methods of reflection. Additional resources are included.

Final Journal

Mark Cooper, author of "The Big Dummy's Guide to Service-Learning," asks questions that facilitate three levels of reflection. You were referred to these questions in step 1 when we talked about journaling. Now you can review your journals and prepare a final version of them, paying more attention to content, detail, writing, and grammar. Here are Mark's questions. Use as many as you would like to create your final journal.

The Mirror: A Clear Reflection of the Self

Who am I?

What are my values?

What have I learned about myself through this experience?

Do I have more or less understanding or empathy than I did before volunteering?

In what ways, if any, have my sense of self, my values, my sense of community, my willingness to serve others, and my self-confidence and self-esteem been affected through this experience?

Have my motivations for volunteering changed? How?

How has this experience challenged my stereotypes or prejudices?

Have I had any realizations or insights, or have you learned any especially strong lessons?

Will these experiences change the way I act or think?

Have I given enough, opened up enough, cared enough?

How have I challenged myself, my ideals, my philosophies, my concept of life, or my way of living?

The Microscope: Makes the Small Experience Large

What happened? Describe your experience.

What would you change about this situation if you could?

What have you learned about this agency, these people, or the community?

Was there a moment of failure, success, indecision, doubt, humor, frustration, happiness, sadness?

Do you feel that your actions had any effect?

What more needs to be done?

Does this experience complement the class material, or does it contrast with it? How?

Has learning through experience taught you more, less, or as much as the class did? In what ways?

The Binoculars: Makes What Is Distant Appear Closer

From your service experience, are you able to identify any issues that are creating or influencing the problem? What can be done to change the situation?

How will this alter your behaviors, attitudes, and career?

How is the issue or agency you're serving affected by the larger political and social conditions?

What does the future hold?

What can be done?

Adapted from M. Cooper, *The big dummy's guide to service-learning: 27 simple answers to good questions on: Faculty, programmatic, student, administration & non-profit issues.* Available: http://www.fiu.edu/~time4chg/Library/bigdummy.html.

An alternative to preparing a final journal is to write a reflection essay where you respond to a series of questions that are designed to encourage reflection.

Reflection Essay

A common reflection format is a reflection essay. If your class chooses this assignment, it should be completed by each student based on what he or she learned throughout the service-learning experience. Your teacher may use or adapt the reflection essay described here so that it appropriate for your class project. An alternative to this essay is for your teacher to give you a more specific series of questions to respond to.

This is a generic assignment format that your class can modify to fit your situation. After each Roman numeral, there is a major heading and a description of what you will write in each section. Ask your teacher which format he or she prefers. Before you begin writing, read your journal entries again. Doing so will help you recall information about your experience.

I. Course understanding. Review the learning objectives that your class set during step 1. Comment on how the project helped you learn the course material related to each objective.

II. Career plans. Write about how your work for the service-learning project has influenced your career plans.

III. Biases and prejudices. Comment on how your experiences during the service-learning project influenced the biases and prejudices you held before the project.

IV. Commitment to making a difference in the community. Comment on how your experiences during this project have influenced your desire to be engaged in community service.

Reflection helps you maximize the benefits of your hard work.

V. Advice for other students. What advice would you offer to a student who might be involved in this service-learning program in the future?

VI. Advice for the teacher. What advice would you offer to a teacher to improve this service-learning assignment?

This is a generic outline format. Your teacher may choose to modify the categories or to give you more questions to respond to that are specific to your service-learning experience.

Program and Self-Evaluation

Stephanie West, a professor at Appalachian State University, recommends that each student evaluate the program and themselves by using this easy-to-follow format created by Drs. West and Siegenthaler for their programming classes. Your Self-Evaluation of Professionalism (table 2.3) and daily journals will serve as good resources as you reflect on personal challenges, on lessons, on your performance, and on the value of the experience and as you make program recommendations.

Prepare a comprehensive review of the project and your performance by writing about each of the following areas. Label each section clearly.

I. Personal challenges. Identify two personal challenges you experienced while developing and implementing the program.

II. Lessons learned. Identify three things you learned while developing and implementing the program.

III. Personal evaluation. Evaluate your performance during the planning and implementation of the program.

IV. Value of the experience. Identify the value of the experience to you both professionally and personally. If you feel that the experience was not personally or professionally valuable, discuss how this situation might be improved for future students.

V. Program recommendations. Make three recommendations for improving the planning or implementation process.

Reprinted, by permission, from S. West, *Program review assignment from course syllabus, Recreation Program Planning.* Appalachian State University, Department of Health, Leisure and Exercise Science.

Another good reflection tool is a reflection portfolio. A portfolio has two benefits—it facilitates reflection, and it leaves you with a product that you can use to showcase your skills to potential employers.

Portfolio

A reflection portfolio is a great way to organize and present evidence of your accomplishments and achievements. The students and teacher can brainstorm together about which items to include. Examples include drafts of documents, completed documents, activity plans, annotated bibliographies, reports, and photos. When individual students make portfolios, they have a finished product that they can present to potential employers.

Presentation

A reflection presentation allows students to talk with others about their accomplishments. Review your accomplishments in steps one through five, and then create a presentation to illustrate how and why you chose your service-learning project, as well as to illustrate what you learned during team building, project planning, project implementation, and celebration. You may want to create a slide show, film or multimedia presentation, or even a Web site to present what your class has accomplished and learned.

Creative Reflection Alternatives

Service-learning expert Cathryn Berger Kaye suggests a variety of methods for eliciting responses to what students learn during service-learning projects—art, poetry, music, role playing, mime, sculpture, drama, movement, and photographs. For example, students can prepare a skit that shows a dilemma they faced during the project. They then ask audience members to step in and respond. Or students can write one or more haiku poems to describe and contemplate a meaningful aspect of their experience. Students might enter class and find a large piece of butcher paper spread out over a table. They would spend 10 minutes drawing and writing about their experience and then discuss the meaning of their illustrations. Students might create poster collages from magazine pictures for the same purpose. Berger provides questions that may help you discuss the meaning of your creative, reflective works.

- What was special about this experience for you?
- What did you learn?
- How did you feel when you were at the service site?
- How did you make a difference?
- Five years from now, what do you think you will remember about this project?
- Consider the class content you covered in preparation for the project. What do you understand better now than you did before?

From C. Berger Kaye, 2003, *The complete guide to service learning: Proven, practical ways to engage students in civic responsibility, academic curriculum, & social action* (Minneapolis, MN: Free Spirit Publishing), 27.

EVALUATIONS, RECORDS, AND RESOURCES

If future classes are to do service-learning projects that are similar to yours, or if they might even work with the same agency, leave good records behind. This will allow the next class to build on your accomplishments rather than to reinvent the wheel. Agencies will appreciate that students are informed about past projects and that they are prepared to improve on them. Leave behind records and recommendations so that your efforts will continue to have a positive influence. Use the following checklist to help you decide on what to leave for future classes:

- ☐ Planning documents
- ☐ Task sheets and a master timeline
- ☐ Photos and videotapes of your event
- ☐ Summary of the challenges faced by the students
- ☐ Summary of the recommendations for future programs
- ☐ List of resources and contacts, with notations about whether they were helpful
- ☐ Best advice. Complete the short activity that follows, and leave the results for the next class.

Best Advice

Your class can share its collective wisdom and experience with others by having each student answer a few questions.

Have each student answer the following questions. Compile them into a single report with clearly labeled sections.

1. Now that I've completed the service-learning project, the one thing I would do differently is . . .
2. Now that I've completed the service-learning project, the one thing I would not do again is . . .
3. If our class were starting over again today, the one thing I would change from the very beginning is . . .

SUMMARY

Congratulations! You have just taken part in something bigger than yourself and have become a better person for it. It's not easy to take part in a complex class project. You've been through everything from choosing a project to team building, planning, implementation, evaluation, and closure. Without each student's talents and contributions, the task could not have been accomplished. Praise yourself and others. Give credit where credit is due. From here you move on to the rest of your education and life experiences. As you carry with you the lessons from this experience, you will continue to touch the lives of others through your service. A final point: To keep what you have gained, you have to give it away. If you continue to serve others, you will continue to grow. Keep up the good work!

REFERENCES

Albert, G. 1996. Intensive service-learning experiences. In B. Jacoby (Ed.), *Service learning in higher education*. San Francisco: Jossey-Bass.

Berger Kaye, C. 2003. *The complete guide to service learning: Proven, practical ways to engage students in civic responsibility, academic curriculum, & social action.* Minneapolis: Free Spirit.

Cooper, M. n.d. The big dummy's guide to service-learning. www.fiu.edu/~time4chg/Library/bigdummy.html.

Rama, D.V., and R. Battistoni. 2001. Service-learning: Using structured reflection to enhance learning from service. www.compact.org/disciplines/reflection/index.html.

Reed, J.C., and Koliba. n.d. Facilitating reflection: A manual for leaders and educators. www.uvm.edu/~dewey/reflection_manual.

RMC Research Corporation. 2003. Connecting thinking and action: Ideas for service-learning reflection. www.servicelearning.org/library/lib_cat/index.php?search_string=%22RMC%22+in+author&library_id=5636.

Shon, D. 1983. The reflective practitioner: How professionals think in action. San Francisco: Jossey-Bass.

STUDENT CHECKLIST

- ☐ Celebration activities planned and completed
- ☐ Reflection activities planned and completed
- ☐ Records and resources compiled and left behind for future students

APPENDIX

Designing Needs Assessment and Evaluation Surveys

A major goal of any service-learning project is to meet people's needs. That's why it's important to understand those needs as you plan and evaluate your project.

When a client's needs are not well defined, a needs assessment survey can help you determine the client's issues. A needs assessment survey helps you gather information about a client's needs, wants, and resources. The purpose of the survey is to gather information that will ensure that your project is valuable to your clients.

It also gathers clients' feedback on your project after the project is finished (see step 4, page 66, for more about using evaluations). You should always conduct an evaluation of your service-learning project. Your project was designed to help people, so you need to know what you did well and what you could have improved. The process of evaluation will help you learn from your experiences and it will provide useful information for any class that might do the same or similar service-learning project in the future.

The information in this appendix is designed to help you assess your needs and evaluate your project. It does this by describing how to write good questions, administer surveys, analyze data, and prepare a report.

As you design your survey, keep in mind the KISS principle: keep it short and simple. People are reluctant to spend time filling out long questionnaires. Questions that they think are too personal or irrelevant will annoy them. The following examples and guidelines will help you design a survey that will yield the information you need to assess your needs and evaluate your service-learning project.

TYPES OF QUESTIONS

There are different types of questions that can be asked in a needs assessment or evaluation survey. It is important to ask only the questions that you need answers to. It is tempting to ask a lot of questions in the hope that you will find something useful. But it is better to carefully consider what you need to know and to limit your survey to those questions.

Demographics

Demographic information describes the age, race, marital status, family status, education, grade in school, employment, income, and place of residence. Some of these questions are personal in nature, so limit the questions to what you truly need to know in order to design or evaluate your program. If people are offended by a question about family income, they may not complete your survey. Avoiding this type of question will be addressed in the section Wording of Questions.

Demographic questions are used to determine whether the people surveyed are representative of the population you want to serve. For example, if your service-learning project is designed to help low-income residents of a particular neighborhood, you need to know whether low-income residents are responding to your survey. It will do no good to survey people at the local mall if most of the respondents do not come from the group you need to know about.

Here is a list of possible demographic questions:

- Age
- Gender
- Racial or ethnic identity
- Religion
- Marital status
- Education level or grade in school
- Self-designated social-class membership
- City or county of residence
- How long the respondent has lived at current residence
- Type of dwelling (owned home, rental home, apartment, group home)
- Zip code or location of residence
- Number and ages of family members
- Grade in school for school-age children
- Type of school attended (public, private, home schooled)
- Racial or ethnic identity of family members
- Annual income of family
- Education of each head of household
- Employment of each head of household

Attitudes, Knowledge, and Beliefs

It might be important to understand what people know, believe, and feel about subjects such as recreation, physical activity, and health practices. Knowledge, beliefs, and attitudes are indicators of what people are motivated to do. While you can educate people through your project, remember that attitudes and beliefs are far more enduring and are less likely to change. Although you can't change a person's attitude, it may still be important to know what she thinks and feels so that you can more easily relate to her.

People base their feelings and their actions on what they know. Thus it's important to find out what a respondent knows before you ask him what he feels or believes about a particular topic. For example, if a person does not know about a particular prenatal-care program, he cannot tell you how he feels about it. You still need to be careful, however, when you ask people about what they know because many people don't like to admit that they don't know something. They may pretend to know about it in order to avoid embarrassment.

To find out what people know about something, you can use either aided or unaided recall (Hudson 1988). With aided recall, you can ask, "Have you ever heard of the Washington Community Center?" or use a checklist with the question "Which of the following programs have you heard of?" To avoid the problem of people saying "yes" even though they have not heard of a place or program, you can use unaided recall. An unaided recall would ask a question such as "Please name a community center that serves senior citizens."

Once you have established which programs and services the respondents know about, you can then ask whether they use them and what they think about them. There are four concepts that can guide your questions (Hudson 1988).

1. What programs the respondents did or did not participate in
2. Where they participated in them
3. When they participated in them
4. How often they participated in them (pp. 15–16)

Examples of the questions you might ask are covered in figure A.1.

If you have used the Community Senior Center, please indicate which programs you used.

1 At least once a week
2 At least once a month
3 At least once every six months
4 Rarely or never participate

Table tennis	1	2	3	4
Water aerobics	1	2	3	4
Yoga	1	2	3	4
Social dance	1	2	3	4
Card games	1	2	3	4

Figure A.1 Sample questions for determining knowledge, participation, and satisfaction.

Needs and Interests

One way to determine your clients' needs and interests is to use open-ended questions such as "What health issues should be better addressed in our community?" If you take this approach, the answers could be so varied that they would be difficult to use. A second approach is to provide a list of ideas for programs or services and to ask people to rate how they feel about each. A third way to assess needs is to ask people which programs they would attend or which services they would use. Consider issues such as cost and location, whether the programs are for the group or individual, and whether the programs are structured or unstructured. Examples of questions you might ask are covered in figure A.2.

Behavior

With regard to recreation, health, or physical activity behaviors, you may want to find out the following:

- What respondents do or do not do at the present time or in the recent past
- Where they participated in the activities
- When they are most likely to participate
- How often they participate in the activities
- Whether they plan to continue with the activities

Examples of questions about current or past behaviors are covered in figure A.3.

Barriers

Respondents often indicate that they would like to participate in a program or service but that something is preventing them from participating. If you can find out what those barriers are and remove some of them, it can dramatically increase the use of these programs and services. Barriers include money, time, transportation, other obligations, or a lack of knowledge about the available programs and services.

Examples of questions regarding reasons why respondents do not or cannot use various programs or services are covered in figure A.4.

Please rate the following health education program ideas according to how much you would like to have this program in your community.

	No desire	Little desire	Neutral	Moderate desire	Strong desire
Walking program					
Nutritional cooking program					
Weight-control program					
Smoking cessation program					

Which of these formats would increase the chance that you would attend a health education program? Check all that would interest you.

	No	Maybe	Yes
Scheduled group class at noon			
Scheduled group class at 5:00 p.m.			
Scheduled group class at 7:00 p.m.			
Distance education via computer			
Individual class or coaching			
Support group meetings			

Figure A.2 Sample questions for assessing the potential needs and interests of the clients.

Please indicate how frequently you do the following activities by placing a check in the appropriate box.

	1 time a week	1 time a month	Every 6 months	Never
Walk on community boardwalk				
Use the parks and recreation fitness facility				
Use the parks and recreation pool				
Attend any parks and recreation scheduled program				

Figure A.3 Sample questions for gathering information about client participation.

There are a variety of reasons why people do not participate in various activities. Please indicate whether any of the following difficulties prevent you from using the health education programs provided by the city of Washington.

Current Health Education Programs

- Weight control
- Nutritional cooking
- Yoga
- Walking
- Smoking cessation

	Not a problem for me	Sometimes a problem	Neutral	Moderate problem	Big problem for me
The cost of the programs is too high.					
The programs are scheduled at a time when I cannot attend.					
I'm too tired to do anything extra.					
I don't know what programs are available.					
I don't know the schedule.					
I don't know how to get there.					
I don't have enough time to do the things I want to do.					
I don't have anyone to go with me.					
I don't really know what I want to do.					

Figure A.4 Sample questions regarding barriers (reasons why respondents do not or cannot use various programs or services).

Satisfaction With Services and Programs

When you conduct an evaluation, you typically want to know whether clients were satisfied with the programs and services you provided. To gather this information, ask the clients to rate each service or program. In addition, ask about overall satisfaction before asking them to rate the specific items in a list. Also, respondents tend to give high ratings to services and programs that they only sort of liked. Using strong language and a wide scale can help you differentiate between what they thought was just okay and what they thought was really good.

Examples of questions about client satisfaction are covered in figure A.5.

The section on evaluation in step 4 contains detailed information on how to gather information about client satisfaction.

WORDING OF QUESTIONS

It is important that the survey questions are clear, unbiased, and unambiguous. Each question should target just one topic. If you ask about two or more topics at once, people may not be able to think of a clear answer.

Consider the following when writing questions for needs assessment and evaluation surveys:

- Use simple words that everyone will understand. For example, instead of asking, "Many people have visited Washington, NC, in the past year to attend Music in the Streets and other festivals. Have you been to the Music in the Streets during the past year?" ask, "Did you attend Music in the Streets in Washington, NC, last year?"
- Use full names and familiar terms instead of using abbreviations or specialized terms that the general public may not know. For example, instead of asking, "What do you believe the social carrying-capacity should be on Topsail Beach?" ask, "How many people do you think it would take to overcrowd the beach?"
- Be as precise and specific as possible. If a question can be answered in more than one way, it will be. For example, instead of asking, "How many hours do you work?" ask, "On average, how many hours do you work each week?"
- Use unbiased language, and avoid leading questions. For example, instead of asking, "Who do you think is most responsible for grade inflation at our university? (a) the students who are demanding higher grades (b) the administration who pushes for higher GPAs (c) the teachers," ask, "Who do you think is most responsible for grade inflation at our university? (a) the students (b) the administration (c) the teachers."
- Do not ask questions that are too personal or that are likely to put respondents on the defensive. Instead allow people to use categories rather than give specific answers. For example, instead of asking, "What is your annual gross income?" ask, "In which of the following ranges is your annual gross income?"
- Ask only one question at a time, and avoid the use of "and," "but," or other conjunctions that link questions together. For example, instead of asking, "Do you use the swimming pool and the

How satisfied were you with the Learn to Swim program? (circle one)

1 Very dissatisfied
2 Dissatisfied
3 Somewhat dissatisfied
4 In the middle, neither satisfied nor dissatisfied
5 Somewhat satisfied
6 Satisfied
7 Very satisfied

	Very dissatisfied						Very satisfied
Quality of swimming instruction	1	2	3	4	5	6	7
Satisfaction with pool facility....................	1	2	3	4	5	6	7
Ease of registration process	1	2	3	4	5	6	7
Value for the price	1	2	3	4	5	6	7

Figure A.5 Examples of questions about client satisfaction.

playground," ask two separate questions. "Do you use the swimming pool?" and "Do you use the playground?"

• Remember to verify that the respondent knows what you are asking about before you ask detailed questions about it. For example, before you ask about a respondent's beliefs, first ask, "Have you ever attended a parks and recreation program?" "If yes, please answer the following questions," and, "If no, go to question 5."

OPEN-ENDED AND CLOSED-ENDED QUESTIONS

An open-ended question gives the respondent no choice of answers. The respondent must think of his or her own answer. For example, "What exercise do you enjoy doing?" forces the respondent to think of an answer. Use an open-ended question when you cannot anticipate how people will respond to your question. Open-ended questions are also used when you want to elicit suggestions or have people give their opinions.

If you consider using open-ended questions on your needs assessment or evaluation, there are a couple of issues to consider. For one, open-ended questions demand more thought from your respondent, and they take a little while to answer. Many people don't want to spend much time filling out a survey, so limit the number of open-ended questions to one or two. Second, it is difficult to categorize and report people's answers to open-ended questions. If you have a lot of surveys, you will have a lot of answers to consider.

Close-ended questions give the respondent choices of answers. For example, if you ask, "How old are you?" you would then provide categories to choose from, such as "under 25," "26 to 35," "36 to 45," "46 to 55," and "over 55 years." You can also make a question partially close-ended by adding an "other" category. Provide a blank space so that respondents can write in their own answer if none of your choices fits their needs.

Most needs assessments and evaluations contain combinations of open- and close-ended questions. A primary consideration is how you plan to use the responses. When you need to quantify (such as count and average) the responses, you will need close-ended questions. When you need to gather opinions or perceptions, you will need to ask open-ended questions so that the respondents can create their own answers.

SCALES

A scale is made up of numbers that are used to quantify the attributes or traits that the researcher wants to measure. Several examples of scales that you can use are included in the figures A.1 through A.5. You should take into account several guidelines for writing a good scale as you design yours.

- Put the choices in order from negative to positive. Respondents are prone to put a check mark next to the first item they read. If you put the most positive item last, it is more likely that they were committed to that positive response.
- In general, use numbers for your scale. Doing so makes the data entry easier later. Check marks are okay if you have a small number of surveys.
- Place the words for what each number means above the numbers so that they are easy to see. Refer to figure A.5 for an example of a partially anchored scale that uses numbers.
- The more numbers you provide—such as a spread of 1 = very dissatisfied and 6 = very satisfied—the more you will be able to distinguish the really good from the mediocre. If you use a shorter spread—such as 1 = not satisfied, 2 = neutral, 3 = satisfied—you won't gather as much information.
- Respondents tend to become frustrated if they are asked to rank 10 items using 1 through 10, with 1 being the highest and 10 the lowest, but not to use any number more than one time. An alternative is to ask them to rate items by priority, such as 1 = top priority, 2 = high priority, 3 = moderate priority, and 4 = low priority. You can calculate the rank yourself using descriptive statistics (covered later).

LENGTH OF SURVEY AND ORDER OF QUESTIONS

If your survey looks too long, is crowded on the page, or seems complicated, people won't fill it out. Here are some techniques you can use to make the respondents more willing to answer your questions.

- Ask only the questions you truly need answers to so that the survey is as short as possible.

- Group your questions by topic, keeping related questions together.
- Use closed-ended questions as much as possible, and add an "other" category if you think that people may have other responses.
- Limit the number of open-ended questions.
- Leave plenty of white space so that the survey does not appear crowded.
- Make sure the directions are clear and obvious.
- Use arrows to guide people through the survey, especially when they need to move to different sections of the survey based on their answer.

PRETESTING THE SURVEY

No one creates a great survey on the first draft. Pretesting the survey is a great way to discover where the problems are. Pretest your survey with at least three groups. If you skip any pretesting step, your survey will almost certainly be flawed. Pretest with each group and make revisions based on the responses.

First, pretest the survey with other students. Your fellow students can look at the appearance of the survey and judge its readability and bias. Other students can help judge whether the survey questions will gather the information you need to meet your objectives.

Second, pretest the survey with the people who will receive the results—meaning the teachers and

Additional Resources for Service-Learning Evaluation

There are several excellent resources that can be consulted if the students and/or teacher want to implement an evaluation that is more in-depth than the one outlined here.

Books

Batenburg, M., D. Clark-Pope. 2000. *The evaluation handbook: Practical tools for evaluating service-learning programs*. Oakland, CA: Service Learning 2000 Center, Youth Service California.

This service-learning evaluation handbook has been written and field-tested with several audiences in mind. Teachers, administrators, students, and advisory boards will find the handbook useful for evaluating a service-learning program. It is both an instruction manual and a workbook that is designed to start you at the beginning and help you build your evaluation plan. Examples of four detailed evaluation tools are included.

Payne, D.A. 2000. *Evaluating service-learning activities and programs*. Lanham, MD: Scarecrow Press.

This e-book helps teachers and researchers determine how service learning relates to their curriculum. This book uses a case-study approach to guide you through the complexities of evaluating service-learning outcomes and determining their relevance to your school's curriculum. The book gives instructions and examples that cover the entire evaluation process, including question formulation, instrumentation, data collection, and application.

Free Internet Resources

- Creative Research Systems (2006) has a survey-design chapter from their tutorial that is reproduced at their Web site and is available to the research community. Retrieve their tutorial on survey design at www.surveysystem.com/sdesign.htm.
- StatPac, Inc., has a free tutorial for designing surveys and questionnaires that you can retrieve at www.statpac.com/surveys.
- Colorado State University's Writing Guides for Survey Research provides an overview of designing written, oral, and electronic surveys, complete with examples. Retrieve these instructions at http://writing.colostate.edu/guides/research/survey.
- The Data Center: Impact Research for Social Justice provides a free guide, "Creating Surveys," that you can download in PDF format. Retrieve this guide at www.datacenter.org/research/creatingsurveys/intro.htm.

project clients. They can tell you if the content of the survey appears to be complete and accurate. They can also help judge whether the survey will gather the desired information.

Third, pretest the survey with some of the respondents themselves. This will show you how long it takes to fill it out, whether the instructions are clear, and whether any wording is confusing.

After the pretest, review everything again. Take out any unnecessary questions, add new categories to closed-ended questions if needed, and make sure that the directions and rating scales are crystal clear. If you have to make major revisions, you should probably pretest the survey again.

ADMINISTERING THE SURVEY

In our age of technology, more and more surveys are being done through e-mail and the Internet. These approaches, however, limit your pool of respondents to persons who have and regularly use these technologies. Since clients who benefit most from service-learning projects may not have easy access to this technology, the focus of this section will be on face-to-face surveys. If you believe that an Internet survey will serve your purposes, look at the Internet resources listed on page 85 for further instructions.

An alternative to a face-to-face survey is a telephone survey. If the group you want to survey is very large and you therefore cannot survey everyone, you will need to learn about sampling methods and sample size. A resource for learning about these concepts is a research-methods textbook. You can find a good explanation of sampling methods at www.statpac.com/surveys/sampling.htm and an electronic calculator at www.surveysystem.com/sscalc.htm.

ANALYZING RESULTS

Most needs assessment and evaluation surveys will require only that you calculate descriptive statistics in order to understand your results. Commonly used descriptive statistics include the following:

- Frequency—how often people choose a particular response
- Percent—what percentage of the respondents choose a particular response
- Mean—the average of all responses
- Standard deviation—the higher the score, the more variable the responses

These basic descriptive statistics can be calculated using Microsoft Excel or the Statistical Package for the Social Sciences (SPSS). Comparing scores between groups using chi square, t tests, and ANOVA [analysis of variance] are beyond the scope of this book, but you can use any basic statistical or research-methods book to learn about these procedures. If you want a helpful book, try the *Complete Idiot's Guide to Statistics* by Bob Donnelly, published by Alpha Books in 2004.

CREATING A REPORT

A report that summarizes the results of a needs assessment or evaluation typically contains the following:

1. **Cover page.** This should have the name of the program, the date of the report, and the names of the people who completed the report.
2. **Summary.** A one-page summary of the report. It allows the reader to understand the context and outcome without reading the entire report.
3. **Background information.** This section might describe the background of the community, the history of the project, and the reasons why the needs assessment or evaluation was conducted.
4. **Description of survey design.** The section on survey design describes how the survey was designed and tested prior to its use.
5. **Results.** The results section presents the descriptive statistics by using tables. An example of a table is shown in figure A.6.
6. **Discussion.** A reflection on the results.
7. **Conclusions and recommendations.** The final section makes conclusions about the results and discussion, and it makes recommendations based on those results.

SUMMARY

The information in this appendix provides an overview of basic information for conducting needs assessments and evaluations. If you plan

How satisfied were you with the Learn to Swim program?

	Frequency	Percent
Very dissatisfied (1)	5	1.1
Dissatisfied (2)	1	.2
Somewhat dissatisfied (3)	5	1.1
In the middle (4)	7	1.6
Somewhat satisfied (5)	27	6.1
Satisfied (6)	124	28.0
Very satisfied (7)	274	61.9
Total respondents	443	100%
Overall mean score	6.42 out of 7.0	
Standard deviation	.62	

Figure A.6 Sample table of results from an evaluation survey.

to conduct one of these surveys, consult additional books about conducting research, needs assessments, and evaluations in your specific area.

If you plan to conduct a survey, find examples of surveys that other students and professionals have used in the past. The results you get will be only as good as the care and effort you put into the survey process. You will probably need only basic survey techniques to evaluate your service-learning project. The information in step 4 and in this appendix will serve you well.

REFERENCES

Hudson, S.D. 1988. *How to conduct community needs assessment surveys in public parks and recreation.* Columbus, OH: Publishing Horizons.

Russell, R.V. 1982. *Planning programs in recreation.* St. Louis: Mosby.

APPENDIX

B

Icebreaker and Diversity-Awareness Activities

This appendix contains three icebreaker and diversity-awareness activities, as well as other strategies, from EdChange, an activist and consultant collaborative dedicated to social justice in schools and communities. Your teacher probably has many books with additional icebreaker activities. When the clients are from a different group from the students (race, socioeconomic status, education levels, age, and so on), however, it will be important to use appropriate icebreaker activities. The third activity in this appendix, Ground Rules, is similar to an activity you will do with your class during the team-building phase. Please note that this activity is relevant in both cases because students need to know their ground rules in order to work well together as a class and because the students and clients need to know how to work well together during the service project.

CHOOSING AND USING ACTIVITIES FOR INTERGROUP LEARNING

As you prepare to conduct your get-to-know-each-other session with the students and clients, you should have a good idea of how many people will come, what you want to accomplish, and how much time you have. Since you may have many activity options to choose from, the following suggestions will help you choose the right ones for your situation. These are suggested by Paul Gorski, who is the founder of EdChange and an assistant professor in the Graduate School of Education at Hamline University.

1. Build a lesson plan around the topics and concepts that the group wants to cover, then design or choose activities for exploring them. Don't build a lesson plan around activities.
2. Choose diverse activities and exercises. Each group of participants will have a range of learning styles and comfort levels with different activities. Some enjoy working in large groups; others prefer to work in pairs. Some like simulations and role playing; others prefer storytelling activities. Try to use ideas from a variety of approaches when designing your plan.
3. The key to intergroup learning is dialogue. Avoid filling the class or workshop with so many activities and exercises that you are left with no time for dialogue and processing.
4. Too often, multicultural or intergroup program designs call for people of color to teach white people about racism, women to teach men about sexism, and so on. Avoid activities that call for oppressed groups to teach privileged groups about their oppression.
5. Whenever possible and appropriate, model a willingness to be vulnerable by participating in class exercises and activities. This can be particularly effective when activities call for sharing stories or personal narratives.

In these cases, you can set the example for the kinds of stories or narratives that you hope others will share.

6. Many diversity activities simulate life through role playing or other experiences in which participants are asked to take on one or more predefined identities. These can be interactive and engaging, but they should be balanced with activities or discussions that draw from the actual experiences of the participants.
7. Films can provide excellent illustrations of concepts, which can lead to fruitful dialogues. But avoid using long films that cut into dialogue time. (Many filmmakers produce two versions of their films—a full-length version and a shorter training version.) In addition, plan how you will transition from watching the film back to discussing the personal experiences of the participants.
8. Be creative. Too often, educators and facilitators become dependent on one or two activities or exercises, but canned activities and exercises are not designed for every context. You have a sense for what will and will not work within yours. Be willing to design new activities or modify existing ones.

Respect

Ask everyone to find someone in the room who they do not know. Ask them to introduce themselves to that person and to spend 5 to 10 minutes talking about respect. For instance, they can discuss the questions "What does it mean to show respect, and what does it mean to be shown respect?" After the allotted time, ask the participants to return to their seats and to discuss the questions as a class.

Common responses to the question include using the golden rule, looking people in the eyes, being honest, and appreciating somebody else's ideas even if you do not agree with him. State that respect is a crucial ingredient in any discussion, but especially in a discussion of multicultural issues. The point is to learn from our differences—to understand each other's understanding. The point is not to agree. Another important part of respect is knowing each other's names and how to pronounce them. Respect also includes keeping the conversation in the group. This type of community building—and the safety that people feel with it—can make or break an attempt to facilitate discussions about multicultural issues.

This activity has several potential benefits. First, it starts the crucial process of building a community of respect. This is the first step in maintaining a constructive exchange about issues such as racism, sexism, and the like. At the most basic level, a participant meets someone he did not know, and he exchanges ideas with that person. Second, the community is built through understanding how the group perceives respect and how they negotiate its meaning. Third, the similarities and differences in everyone's ideas about respect begin to appear.

Who I Am

To increase awareness and encourage self-development, engage participants in activities that call for introspection and self-reflection. Also provide opportunities for participants to make connections across, and even within, cultural lines as participants discover unexpected similarities and differences between themselves and others in the group. This activity is a safe way for students to think about and share the influences that have shaped them.

This activity can also be an excellent last activity, allowing folks to reconnect at the end of an experience in which they are discussing difficult issues.

Ask participants to take 10 to 15 minutes to write a poem called "Who I Am." Instruct them that the only rule for the piece is that each line must start with the phrase "I am . . . " Give them as much leeway as possible, but suggest that they can, if they wish, include statements about their regional, ethnic, religious backgrounds, memories from different points in their lives, interests and hobbies, mottos or credos, favorite phrases, family traditions and customs, and whatever else defines who they are. Be sure to let them know that they will be sharing their poems.

To ensure that everybody has an opportunity to share her or his story, you might consider breaking the large group into smaller groups of 8 to 10 people. Give participants the option of either reading their poems or sharing parts of their poems from memory.

Here are some points to remember:

1. Because someone includes personal information, she might be hesitant to read her poems, even in a small group. It is sometimes effective in such situations for facilitators to share their poems first. Consider sharing your poem before asking the students to write their own. If you make yourself vulnerable, others will be more comfortable doing the same.
2. Be sure to allow time for everyone to share their poems.
3. If you're using this activity as a final activity, not much processing is necessary. Encourage applause, and thank everyone for sharing their poetry.
4. If you use this activity in the middle of a class or workshop, have some process questions ready. After everyone has read their poems, ask participants how it felt to share them.
5. Ask what, if any, connections people made with each other through this activity. Were there any common themes among the poems? Did any of these surprise you?
6. You might consider asking people to talk to someone who they felt a connection with through the poetry.

This is my "Who I Am" poem:

I am a basketball on a snowy driveway.

I am fishsticks, crinkle-cut frozen french fries, and frozen mixed vegetables.

I am primarily white, upper-middle-class neighborhoods, and racially diverse schools.

I am Donkey Kong, Ms. Pac Man, Atari 2600, and sports video games.

I am football on Thanksgiving and New Year's Day.

I am "unity in diversity" and "speaking from your own experience."

I am triple-Wahoos, earning three degrees from the University of Virginia.

I am diversity, multicultural education, identity, introspection, self-reflection, and social action.

I am Daffy Duck, Mr. Magoo, Hong Kong Phooey, Foghorn Leghorn, and other cartoons.

I am taekwondo, basketball, the batting cages, a soccer family, and the gym.

I am a wonderful family, close and loving and incredibly supportive.

I am films based on true stories and documentaries.

I am the History Channel, CNN, ESPN, Bravo, and Home Team Sports.

I am a passion for educating and facilitating, personal development, and making connections.

Ground Rules

Whenever you hope to facilitate conversations about multicultural issues, whether preparing for a one-hour workshop or weaving discussions into a yearlong class, a vital first step is developing participation guidelines. These guidelines, often referred to as ground rules, should ensure open, respectful dialogue and maximum participation.

There are several ways to create ground rules. If time is an issue, as it tends to be in short workshops of one to two hours, it may be necessary for you to simply list the ground rules for the group. Be sure to ask whether everyone agrees to the ground rules, and mention that if you had more time together, you would have preferred that the group generate the list.

A second way to create ground rules is to list the rules you commonly use and then to ask for additional rules from the participants. When someone proposes a new rule, ask the other participants if they agree to it. If most do, add it to the list.

The best way to create ground rules, if you have the time, is to allow the participants to generate the entire list. Ask them how each of them can ensure a safe environment to discuss difficult and controversial issues. If the participants are having difficulty coming up with ground rules, or if they do not think of a particular ground rule that you feel is important to the success of your facilitation, try to prompt them toward it. If they still do not mention it, you can suggest adding it to the list.

Ground rules should be developed and adapted for each context. Appropriate ground rules may depend partially on age, region, social class, and other contextual factors. The following list of common ground rules from multicultural education classes and workshops should serve only as a starting point:

1. Listen actively—respect others when they are talking.
2. Speak from your experience instead of generalizing (use "I" instead of "they," "we," and "you").
3. Arrive on time for class.
4. Do not be afraid to respectfully challenge one another by asking questions, but refrain from personal attacks. Focus on ideas.
5. Participate to the fullest of your ability—community growth depends on the inclusion of every voice.
6. Instead of invalidating somebody else's story with your spin on his or her experience, just share your story and experience.
7. The goal is not to agree; it is to hear and explore divergent perspectives.
8. Be conscious of body language and nonverbal responses; they can be as disrespectful as words.

It is also important to set rules for managing the discussion. Should participants raise their hands and be called on, or should people speak freely? Remember that some people—especially those who tend to be introverted—need time to process their thoughts and to speak; so the latter option may exclude them from the discussion. Then again, the formal process of raising hands to be recognized may detract from an informal atmosphere that might be necessary for discussing multicultural issues.

Here are a few more strategies and notes to consider:

1. Post the ground rules in an obvious location for the duration of the service-learning project. Sometimes teachers or facilitators who are with a certain group for an extended time will bring the list of ground rules (on news print or on some other transportable medium) back to the group for every session or class period. They can then refer back to the list when they sense that participants are not sufficiently following one or more of the items.
2. Challenge the participants on the ground rules early and often. If you do not set a tone of strict adherence to the rules early in the process, it may be impossible to enforce them later.
3. If you use more than two or three ground rules, try focusing on a particular rule during the appropriate activity or discussion. For example, if you are leading the discussion of a large group, state before the

discussion starts that you would like to focus on active listening. Challenge participants to refrain from having any side discussions. Another way to encourage active listening during an experiential activity is to have everyone be silent during it.

4. You must *model* these ground rules in your participation. This is especially true for a guideline such as speaking from your experience. Be sure that your language reflects ownership and responsibility by using as many "I" and "me" statements as possible.
5. If a particular ground rule is routinely broken, make the participants aware of it. A fruitful discussion can often arise from an examination of why the participants are not adhering to particular rules.
6. Revisit the ground rules occasionally, and if time allows, ask whether the participants would like to add any new ones.

Index

Note: The italicized *f* and *t* following page numbers refer to figures and tables, respectively.

About the Author

Cheryl A. Stevens, PhD, is an associate professor at East Carolina University in Greenville, North Carolina. She has 20 years of experience in experiential education, organizational development, and teaching in the disciplines of recreation and leisure foundations, outdoor leadership, and environmental science. Stevens also worked as an organizational development specialist for the City of Anaheim, California.

As a committed experiential educator, Stevens has incorporated service learning as an essential element in many recreation courses. Her inspiration for the book came after instructing a course that involved a highly complex service-learning project. With the goals of student success and involvement in mind, Stevens combined her knowledge and experience in leadership, team building, and organizational development in designing the book's step-by-step process.

Stevens is a member of the National Recreation and Park Association (NRPA), where she currently serves as a member of the Council on Accreditation (COA). She is also a member of the Society of Park and Recreation Educators (SPRE), the Association for Experiential Education, and the North Carolina Recreation and Park Association (NCRPA).

A distinguished educator, Stevens has been repeatedly honored for her innovative teaching methods. In 2002, she received the University Award for Outstanding Teaching from East Carolina University. In 2003, Stevens received an Innovation in Teaching Award from the Society for Park and Recreation Educators and the UNC Board of Governors Distinguished Professor for Teaching Award from East Carolina University. She was also recipient of the College of Health and Human Performance Outstanding Teacher Award from East Carolina University in 2004.

Stevens resides in Washington, North Carolina. In her free time, she enjoys kayaking, gardening, and playing with her dogs.